Arguments for a theatre
Second edition

Howard Barker's reputation as a major European dramatist has been forged over 20 years' work both in major state theatres like the Royal Shakespeare Company, and in the independent theatres, particularly through The Wrestling School, an innovative company dedicated to the performance of his work. Always controversial, Barker's drama makes demands on its audience as a first principle; it is characteristically tragic, poetic, emotional, and by the imaginative power of its situations and the metaphor and poetry of its form, draws theatre beyond its conventional range. Over a period of years Barker has moved towards defining his aims and methods, beginning with the now celebrated manifesto *Fortynine asides* in 1985. His strategy is to change the habitual relations between stage and audience, to encourage a different way of experiencing theatre, and to liberate its particular strengths from ideological restrictions which have aggregated over years of Stanislavskian and Brechtian practice.

In this collection of essays, lectures, aphorisms, Barker elaborates his concept of a Theatre of Catastrophe, a form of tragedy without reconciliation, and locates his expectations in the experience of theatre rather than its moral content. Also here are short, searching pieces on individual performances by actors, notes on productions, drawings and poems which are oblique but illuminating reflections on a changing theory.

Howard Barker's best-known plays are *Scenes from an Execution*, *The Castle*, *The Possibilities*, *The Bite of the Night*, and *The Europeans*.

Arguments for a theatre

Second edition

Howard Barker

Manchester University Press
Manchester and New York

distributed exclusively in the USA and Canada by St. Martin's Press

First published 1989 by John Calder (Publishers) Ltd.
This edition published by Manchester University Press
Oxford Road, Manchester M13 9PL, UK
and Room 400, 175 Fifth Avenue, New York, NY 10010, USA

Distributed exclusively in the USA and Canada by
St. Martin's Press, Inc., 175 Fifth Avenue, New York,
NY 10010, USA

British Library Cataloguing-in-Publication Data
A catalogue record for this book is available from the British Library

Library of Congress Cataloging-in-Publication Data
Barker, Howard,
Arguments for a theatre/Howard Barker, — 2nd ed.
p.   cm.
Includes bibliographical references.
ISBN 0–7190–3997–5. — ISBN 0–7190–3998–3 (pbk.)
1. Theater. 2. Theater and society. 3. English drama-History
and criticism. I. Title.
PN2038.B27   1993   93–3539
792—dc20

ISBN 0 7190 3997 5 *hardback*
0 7190 3998 3 *paperback*

Typeset by J&L Composition Ltd, Filey, North Yorkshire

Printed in Great Britain
by Bell & Bain Limited, Glasgow

Contents

I

Introduction to the second edition

Howard Barker has, over the past two decades, produced a large body of work, comprising for the main part plays but also including in its span several volumes of poetry and numerous essays on the nature and function of contemporary theatre. He has always defied categorization, his work refusing to fit snugly into schools of thought or artistic movements, but this very quality of work, which defines itself in terms of opposition and refusal, has earned him over the years the generic title of a 'difficult' writer. That his output is complex and demanding is beyond question, and it is not my intention to ease or smooth out the complexity which characterizes his writing, for it is this quality which has consistently produced a passionate response, both by admirers who welcome his density of thought and eddying articulation of the forbidden and by his detractors who charge him with wilful obscurantism and arrogant elitism. Where the opposing factions find common ground is in an appreciation of Barker's exciting and often startling work as a playwright, born of the need to create a theatre form unique to the audience which seeks it out.

The question which haunts not only the essays included in this volume, but also – and most pronouncedly – the plays written by Barker throughout the 1980s and into the 1990s, concerns the specific nature of artistic engagement initiated by the writer of dramatic texts. In a poem, 'To the Aberystwyth students', he attempts to articulate the temper of his creative demands:

> We gather round a text which yields
> Meaning reluctantly
> We try to perform the contradiction
> We do not smooth and it occurs
>
> That must be the purpose of art
> That must be art occurring
> Its discomfort is considerable
> And yet we return[1]

For the spectator, actor or director approaching Barker's work, the task specified by the playwright is not one of acquiescence, acceptance or passive reception. The pact he forges demands rather an active engagement of intransigent will 'grinding on the complexity of the text' until individual meaning is forged out of the exigencies of the struggle.

Barker's interrogation of the role of the playwright and the nature and status of the art he produces is specific to the period in which he finds himself writing for the theatre. The crisis he perceives to characterize the contemporary British stage threatens the extinction not only of the artists who work within its sphere but also of the audience it serves. Without acknowledgement of this crisis the whole corpus of theatrical endeavour is in danger of becoming a corpse to which we give the last rites in empty auditoria.

In order to engage fully in the debate to which Barker gives voice in the following pages, it may be helpful to recall Roland Barthes's seminal essay 'The Death of the Author' (1977). This essay marks a similar crisis in the field of literary production and denounces the liberal humanist text, identified as the edifice of establishment literary endeavour, for its inability to maintain the 'truths' it purports to endow upon its reader. Barthes's central proposition is that once the text is refused as a theological utterance, concomitant to the refusal of the Author/God as the central organizing agent of truth, then the linear construction of narrative and the functioning of characters within that narrative are exposed as an ideological means of excluding the reader from active engagement with the fragmented and often contradictory components which make up the text. If this ideological 'cement' remains concealed, the reader is designated a role outside the text, hugging its contours and acted upon as a passive recipient of its 'message' or 'truth'. The only access allowed to such a reader is via a psychological empathy with characters within the text, and the only judgement invited is that which is based upon the moral precepts which the text explores. This reader is, therefore, totally subordinate to the organization of meaning preferred by the author, and the unity or wholeness of the finished text presupposes an authorial ownership of the concepts therein.

Barthes proposes that the 'death' of the Author/God as an ideological category (which carries with it the bourgeois baggage of ownership and property) will expose the text to its proper function, as a multi-dimensional space in which a variety of meanings, 'truths'

[4]

and ideologies, none of which bears the burden of absolute truth, ✓ clash, contradict and juxtapose themselves. The reader who will be born out of the demise of authorial originality and organization will find himself positioned differently with regard to the text. Instead of being excised from its wholeness, the reader will be wedged between the cracks of its fractures, filling its absence with cognitive presence and making complete, through the nature of his active engagement, that which would remain incomplete without him.

Adrian Page in *The Death of the Playwright* (1992) addresses Barthes's assault upon the authority of the author and examines its relevance to the sphere of theatrical production. For Page, there is an important distinction to be made between the hypothetical author, writing in isolation and presenting his unmediated work to a faceless reader, and the playwright, whose work is subjected to interpretation and dramatic mediation before being presented to a mass audience. He asserts that for this reason alone the theatre as an institution has long since ceased to regard the playwright as 'the ultimate source of the text's meaning'.

For Page, the institutional structures which support the production of a playwright's work are important factors in the decentring of the text's originary 'truth'. He asserts that the process undergone by a text on its journey to the stage is more a transformation than a reflection or reproduction of the author's written word. Thus, the exposure of a text to a second signifying system, one which involves the creation of an interpretation by actors and director in order to make the work 'live', constitutes a translation of the text from its original language to the vocabulary of stage performance. The playwright's work becomes, therefore, a stimulus, or blueprint from which a living form emerges: a 'simulacrum' of reality which provides the spectator with a freedom of interpretation equal to that which operates outside the theatre.

In Page's model, the theatre spectator is guaranteed the freedom to interpret what he sees, knowing the performance to be a representation only of the text's blueprint, but remains a passive recipient subject to an alternative unity and a secondary authoring: that of the director. Thus the audience member may judge between versions of a text, but remains ultimately impotent as an autonomous agent of meaning.

For Barthes, the ideology of authorship reaches beyond the

physical entity of the author; it defines any attempt to appropriate meaning and offer that meaning as an objective truth. It is not enough therefore to pose the question 'Is the author telling the truth?': one has to reach beyond the proposition that truth exists, beyond the categories of reason which defend the right to truth and into the hinterland of uncertainty, ambiguity and doubt: what Howard Barker calls 'the pain of unknowing'.

As a prerequisite to the engendering of the critical and creative spectator, Barker recognizes the responsibility of the author, or playwright, to be the interrogation and fragmentation of his own ideological identity. To this end, Barker utilizes the convention of the prologue in his play *The Bite of the Night* (1988), in order to address the audience directly, not as a figure of omnipotent authorship, but as a fractured voice characterized by ambiguity and uncertainty. His theatrical method determines to show not the author's destination, but rather the process of struggle which initiates artistic endeavour. First, the refusal of ideological identity:

> Clarity
> Meaning
> Logic
> And Consistency
>
> None of it
> None[2]

And then the promise

> I'll take you
> I'll hold your throat
> I will
> And vomit I will tolerate
> Over my shirt
> Over my wrists
> Your bile
> Your juices
> I'll be your guide
> And whistler in the dark
> Cougher over filthy words
> And all known sentiments recycled for this house.[3]

The only certainty Barker offers his spectator is that he will not purport to tell the truth. The theatrical experience offered to the audience becomes therefore a mutual striving for meaning, a process

of 'birthing' in which both parties are required to plunge their minds
beyond the mannered responses of ideological category and recognition, and into the guts and viscera of theatrical gestation. Thus, the
spectator is invited to witness and assist the pains of labour, rather
than admire the new-born child.

The Bite of the Night may be singled out in the body of work
Barker has produced to date because it marks a turning point in his
dramatic method; this, and the plays which follow, challenge un-
ceasingly the edifice of authorship and seek to reclaim the theatre as
an arena for imaginative speculation. This task involves no less than
the shattering of theatre as an institutional edifice and the emergence
from its ruins of a new theatre and a new spectator.

Each of the arguments offered in this volume articulates the need
to explore beyond what we know and expect of theatre. They speak
the desire to probe beyond the certainties of narrative and the
psychological nuances of character. His work may be likened to a
process of demolition which reveals, in the eerie calm and settling
dust which follows blasting, the raw material out of which new
structures may be built.

The settings of Barker's later plays are, therefore, panoramas of
desolation, reflecting the ravaged landscape of the ideological battle-
field. The solid structures and inviolable edifices which characterized
the setting of the naturalistic play give way to crumbling and
shattered remnants, standing as testimony to willed destruction. The
characters which traverse this landscape are refugees from a world
which once seemed to offer them reason and purpose; as the
structures atrophy around them, so does their ability to give their
lives coherent meaning. Out of the pain of their loss emerges an
imperative: the need to forge new meanings out of the fractured ruins
of their identity.

In Barker's play *The Europeans* (1990) the birthing of the spectator
as author of his own meaning is demonstrated as requiring the
prerequisite of a crisis of meaning or breakdown of moral consensus.
The Habsburg Emperor Leopold returns triumphant from his routing
of the Turks to a war-ravaged Vienna. Refusing the imperative to
reconstruction, as a symbol of the conquering spirit, he embraces the
stasis of a city in ruins which represents what Victor Turner has
described as 'the liminal':

> the 'subjunctive mood' of culture, the mood of maybe, might be, as-if,
> hypothesis, fantasy, conjecture, desire . . . Liminality can be perhaps

[7]

described as a fructile chaos, a fertile nothingness, a storehouse of possibilities, not by any means a random assemblage, but a striving after new forms and structure.[4]

Situated in his still ruined palace, symbolic of the fractured nature of the era, he invites for conference an assembly of critics from the Academy of Art. Surrounded by the decaying artefacts of a defunct world order, he insists upon their recognition of the crisis out of which new forms and structures will be born. Thus, he demands of the gathered assembly the defining principles which should constitute a new art in a new Europe:

LEOPOLD. Not the room as we would want it. Not the salon we would choose, the swags being somewhat chipped and the putti lacking gilt, but in such pock-marked landscapes imagination might erupt, I call upon you to elucidate the principles of a new art, because the stir of Europe from its sleep commands a terrible and unrelenting movement of the soul.[5]

Leopold calls for an art born of the imaginative impulses forged in a liminal landscape of transition. This art is to be conceived not from the rational impulses of literary form or historical documentation, but from the 'fructile chaos' of possibilities lurking in the surrounding desolation, and the magnificent imperative of the imaginative consciousness to erupt out of the pain which it has witnessed. In answer to his call the salon plunges into a chaos of conflicting ideologies. Refusing Leopold's request for an art which will mediate the pain of crisis, they offer him instead art as a solution to pain. Thus, art is offered as a salve to the wounds inflicted by the war, as a remedy for the obstacles preventing reconstruction, and as a form of 'truth' through which the heterogeneous fragments of the shattered State may be made whole. These 'experts' of artistic endeavour demonstrate their predilection for art as reconciliation, hatching fully-formed the artistic conventions which would service their ideological crusade.

As sole spectator to the critics' antics, Starhemberg, the leader of the campaign against the Turks, comments upon the absurdity of their designs, and likens the spectacle they present to that of a snake split into seven segments frantically attempting to reconstruct itself. Faced with a spectator who resolutely refuses to applaud their appropriation of reality and need, the assembly require of Starhemberg a definition which would constitute the new art. He replies, but only after asserting that his remarks issue from an individual and wholly untrustworthy need predicated upon the imperative of the 'I' as opposed to the 'We':

> STARHEMBERG. What I need. And what there will be. I need an art which will recall pain. The art that will be will be all flourishes and celebration. I need an art that will plummet through the floor of consciousness and free the unborn self. The art that will be will be extravagant and dazzling. I need an art that will shatter the mirror in which we pose. The art that will be will be all mirrors. I want to make a new man and a new woman but only from the pieces of the old. The new man and the new woman will insist on their utter novelty. I ask a lot. The new art will ask nothing.[6]

Starhemberg refuses art, either as a panacea or as camouflage to the pain he as an individual experiences. As a spectator to historical schism, he demands an art form which will shatter the categories of ideological belief and expose the painful wounds which such belief conceals. His needs institute the right of the spectator to share the author's journey, as equal and not subordinate to the ordering of perception and experience. This new spectator, traversing an un-mapped terrain, with rights of refusal and astonishment intact, does not move towards a predetermined destination or synthetic whole-ness but rather embraces the chaos of 'not-knowing' which liberates the imagination from its stranglehold of utilitarian purposefulness, into the possibility of what Barker calls 'the unlived life': that which is defined by individual desire and exists only in the margins of socialized behaviour.

Starhemberg is described as 'a cold and wonderfully imagined man'; he is a man who, in refusing to be 'authored', has created himself out of his own imagination. This process of self 'invention' forms the major thrust of Barker's later plays. It is a process which is posited in opposition to the self which is 'discovered'. To 'discover' oneself has been a major preoccupation of the twentieth century; psychoanalysis, therapy and the major body of artistic expression have progressed the liberal-humanist notion that beneath the surface of everyday activity exists an essentialism which for the most part remains hidden from view, but which makes sense of that which may appear arbitrary and lacking in unity. The mundane round of daily life is thus compensated for by the notion that a profound interiority lurks behind our every action, needing only the correct stimulus to unfold before the waiting subject a hitherto unsuspected vista of subjective possibilities. The process of discovery, however, lies in the hands of professionals who lead the awakened self through its journey of enlightenment, charting its progress with a carefully defined vocabulary which functions as a map to unfamiliar terrain. The discovered man is thus in no way free from the play of significations which determine, or author, social being; rather he stakes the self against a range of discourses which offer profundity of being at the expense of autonomous determination. The discoverers of the self are concerned to produce evidence of origin; the inventors of the self know the unifying self to be a fiction, and therefore strive to consciously create themselves as a work of art.

In Howard Barker's forthcoming version of Chekhov's *Uncle Vanya* (1993), the playwright determines to save the central character, Vanya, from his authored existence as a device within the Chekhovian narrative:

> In rescuing Vanya from resentment I lent him no solution, since there is no solution to a life. My Vanya is however, cleansed of bad blood, his actions liberated from the sterile calculations of the pleasure-principle, and his will to self-creation triumphant over guilt.[7]

The structures by which Barker perceives Vanya to be imprisoned within the text comprise a narrative which celebrates 'paralysis and spiritual vacuity', a psychological rendering of character which diminishes by making sense of Vanya's tempestuous and irrational anger and the creation of a naturalist form which, in its reproduction of the rhythms of 'lived life', denies the imaginative breadth of the human spirit. In making as its cornerstone pity for its central character, Barker asserts that Chekhov's text appeals to a death-wish inherent in the spectator: the desire to limit and entrap the imagination within firmly fixed boundaries of action and response. The conventions which inform the Chekhovian text are, therefore, inducements to atrophy of the spectator's will to imagine.

Barker's version of *Uncle Vanya* removes the constrictions of the naturalist form and allows the characters to comment upon, and question, the art form to which they have been made complicit:

SEREBRYAKOV.   We reverence him because
We reverence Chekhov
Because in such a confined space the melancholy of
Not tragedy
The melancholy of

> Our unlived life is exquisitely redeemed
> We are forgiven
> We are forgiven.[8]

Vanya himself recognizes that his freedom lies not in the redemption offered by the Author/God but in the transformational quality of his anger which, if expressed according to the parameters of his desire, will take his character beyond the pitiable 'apotheosis of self denial' towards a representation of that which is unforgivable, and therefore immune to moral justification. To this end, Barker allows what is censored by Chekhov, the uniting of Vanya with the object of his desire, Helena. Their union is not, however, allowed to rest upon the mutual gratification of sexual fulfilment, but rather upon a love born of the painful need to escape the cyclical entrenchments of narrative resolution. As the structures and conventions which characterize Chekhov's text begin to crumble, exposing in their wake the chaos of moral speculation which their certainties have sought to disguise, the author himself is drawn to the site of the text, buffeted on the waves of a metaphorical ocean which threatens to submerge the last vestiges of clarity and reason clinging like driftwood to the increasingly fragmented characters of the play. As Chekhov confronts the battered remnants of his form, Serebryakov poses a question:

> We know what a play is but what is an author?
> The author also sins
> The author is not very clean
> Is he clean
> I often wonder.[9]

The ensuing dialogue reveals Vanya to be the symptom of his creator's disease, the carrier of an infection which threatens the health of those who are exposed to its contagious fumes. This illness, born of an erosion of the will to confront moral uncertainty, drains its symptomatic art forms of their urgent need to express that which is inexpressible, to define the boundaries by which art is marked off from real life in its inexhaustible quest for the forms by which the imagination may find its way into the public arena. In Chekhov's *Uncle Vanya*, the imagination has become a shameful thing, couched in the recesses of the sub-text and hidden from the public view; Barker exposes the possibilities of the imaginative impulse prioritizing its effects beyond the exigencies of plot and character formation.

[11]

Barker's Chekhov, having demonstrated his skills in the delimiting of the human will and negation of imaginative possibilities, requests a final moment with the diminished Vanya of his creation. In recognizing the disease he has become, he attempts to sound its origins:

> CHEKHOV. One day I hoped I would reach out and tell myself, pour myself like a liquid from a jug into the void of another, all, entire, to the last drop, how I struggled with this dream to pour myself into another man! A woman! To be drained . . . ! And in abandoning that dream I found something like freedom. In discarding all that was arguably, the best in me, I found a peace of sorts.[10]

Barker's Chekhov, having found his peace at the expense of the characters – and by implication the spectators – he has created, is subjected to a Barthesian demise. Confronted with the lifeless form of their erstwhile oppressor, the remnants of the Chekhovian world hover in the liminal space of their potential liberation. Chekhov's characters, now freed from ideological representations of truth, find themselves shipwrecked and clinging to the flotsam and jetsam of the ravaged naturalist form. With only pain for sustenance they attempt reconstruction and settle uneasily into a fractured form which, whilst denying the articulacy and coherence of the Chekhovian original, still retains echoes of his creation. Only Vanya, whose intense anger accelerates his actions beyond any form of reconciliation with his genesis, finds the will to quit 'the Chekhovian madhouse', thus becoming, in the words of his new creator, 'a metaphor for the potential of art to point heroically, if blindly, to the open door'.

The final stage-direction offered in Barker's version of *Uncle Vanya* precludes any possibility of Vanya's return to the space of his gestation. What lies beyond the open door is still to be determined, but Barker issues an invitation to the spectator to participate in a journey towards a new definition of theatre which at once makes great demands upon tolerance and individual sensibility, but also centralizes the role of the audience member in determining and demanding the forms which will satisfy the potential for the imaginative involvement inherent in artistic engagement.

Howard Barker's later plays are divisive, eschewing the myth of collective response within the theatre. As prerequisite to the emergence of a new art, he redefines the playwright as 'a sinner', one who struggles to expose the full breadth of imaginative expression, beyond the bounds of conscience and expatiated guilt. The spectators for his art are born of an act of faith: his belief that beyond the gratuitous play of supply and demand which characterizes the culture industry, there exists a desire to explore the un-authored life.

In *Laws,* the philosopher Plato observes the imagination to be a dangerous tool in the hands of artists, for in its free play of contradiction and love of ambiguity it tests the unity of individual identity, exposing the possibility that the same part of us may hold different opinions about the same thing at the same time. Recognizing the explosive potential inherent in imaginative play, he counsels:

> If you control the way children play, and the same children always play the same games under the same rules and in the same conditions, and get pleasure from the same toys, you'll find that the conventions of adult life too are left in peace without alteration.[11]

In *Arguments for a theatre* Barker questions the need for guardianship and counsels the spectator to insist upon his right to come of age.

Amanda Price is a lecturer in Theatre Studies at The Workshop Theatre, University of Leeds.

Notes

1 Howard Barker, *Gary the Thief/Gary Upright* (Calder, 1987), pp. 86–7.
2 Howard Barker, *The Bite of the Night* (Calder, 1988), p. 3.
3 Barker, *ibid.*, p. 3.
4 Victor Turner, 'Are there Universals of Performance?' in *By Means of Performance*, ed. Richard Schechner & Willa Appel (Cambridge, 1990), p. 12.
5 Howard Barker, *The Europeans* (Calder, 1990), p. 28.
6 Barker, *ibid.*, p. 31.
7 Howard Barker, *Uncle Vanya* in *Collected Plays*, vol. 2 (Calder, 1993).
8 *Ibid.*
9 *Ibid.*
10 *Ibid.*
11 Plato, *Laws*, 797.

Works cited

Barthes, Roland, 'The Death of the Author' in *Image-Music-Text*, essays selected and translated by Stephen Heath (Fontana, 1977).
Page, Adrian (ed.), *The Death of the Playwright?* (Macmillan, 1992).

II

Fortynine asides for a tragic theatre*

We are living the extinction of official socialism. When the opposition loses its politics, it must root in art.

The time for satire is ended. Nothing can be satirized in the authoritarian state. It is culture reduced to playing the spoons. The stockbroker laughs, and the satirist plays the spoons.

The authoritarian art form is the musical.

The accountant is the new censor. The accountant claps his hands at the full theatre. The official socialist also hankers for the full theatre. But full for what?

In an age of populism, the progressive artist is the artist who is not afraid of silence.

The baying of an audience in pursuit of unity is a sound of despair.

In a bad time laughter is a rattle of fear.

How hard it is to sit in a silent theatre.

There is silence and silence. Like the colour black, there are colours within silence.

The silence of compulsion is the greatest achievement of the actor and the dramatist.

We must overcome the urge to do things in unison. To chant together, to hum banal tunes together, is not collectivity.

A carnival is not a revolution.

After the carnival, after the removal of the masks, you are precisely who you were before. After the tragedy, you are not certain who you are.

Ideology is the outcome of pain.

Some people want to know pain. There is no truth on the cheap.

* First published in *The Guardian*, 10 February 1986.

[17]

There are more people in pursuit of knowledge than the accountants will admit.

There is always the possibility of an avalanche of truth-seekers.

Art is a problem. The man or woman who exposes himself to art exposes himself to another problem.

It is an error typical of the accountant to think there is no audience for the problem.

Some people want to grow in their souls.

But not all people. Consequently, tragedy is elitist.

Because you cannot address everybody, you may as well address the impatient.

The opposition in art has nothing but the quality of its imagination.

The only possible resistance to a culture of banality is quality.

Because they try to debase language, the voice of the actor becomes an instrument of revolt.

The actor is both the greatest resource of freedom and the subtlest instrument of repression.

If language is restored to the actor he ruptures the imaginative blockade of the culture. If he speaks banality he piles up servitude.

Tragedy liberates language from banality. It returns poetry to speech.

Tragedy is not about reconciliation. Consequently, it is the art form for our time.

Tragedy resists the trivialization of experience, which is the project of the authoritarian regime.

People will endure anything for a grain of truth.

But not all people. Therefore a tragic theatre will be elitist.

Tragedy was impossible as long as hope was confused with comfort. Suddenly tragedy is possible again.

When a child fell under a bus they called it a tragedy. On the contrary, it was an accident. We have had a drama of accidents masquerading as tragedy.

The tragedies of the 1960s were not tragedies but failures of the social services.

The theatre must start to take its audience seriously. It must stop telling them stories they can understand.

It is not to insult an audience to offer it ambiguity. ✓

The narrative form is dying in our hands.

In tragedy, the audience is disunited. It sits alone. It suffers alone.

In the endless drizzle of false collectivity, tragedy restores pain to the individual.

You emerge from tragedy equipped against lies. After the musical, ✓ you are anyone's fool.

Tragedy offends the sensibilities. It drags the unconscious into the public place. It therefore silences the banging of the tambourine which characterizes the authoritarian and the labourist culture alike.

It dares to be beautiful. Who talks of beauty in the theatre any more? ✓ They think it is to do with the costumes.

Beauty, which is possible only in tragedy, subverts the lie of human squalor which lies at the heart of the new authoritarianism.

When society is officially philistine, the complexity of tragedy becomes a source of resistance.

Because they have bled life out of the word freedom, the word justice attains a new significance. Only tragedy makes justice its preoccupation.

Since no art form generates action, the most appropriate art for a culture on the edge of extinction is one that stimulates pain.

The issues are never too complex for expression.

It is never too late to forestall the death of Europe.

Ye gotta laugh*

1

We grew ashamed of the I in the theatre and learned to talk of the We. Rightly, because the art is collective, and because we were doing new things, rapidly making enemies.

I also wanted to belong, and found at once the actors were the allies who knew by speaking what struck and what missed better than the managers, who are careerists or idealists, or writers, who follow each other.

I sensed the authority of the spoken word but still did not grasp its range, its arc of effect in a culture frantic with images, fevered with pictures and products, visually sick.

The word was deliberately maimed, pulped into headline or spewed into naturalistic loops. Speech, as art, was spattered with a double contempt, by the left who required workers to grunt and the right, who were coming to the masses at last, levelling princesses to the suburban mode.

When the politics broke, the We was lost in the tide. The culture, nakedly cannibalistic, lent authority to despair, made a ground for archaic theologies and permitted philistinism to parade as democratic art.

The managers leapt to sham renaissance postures, wanting power, gold, and spectacle, while the fringe, which had sheltered even those whose aesthetic was not oppositional, suffered a double relapse, a miniaturist art no longer fitting the ambition of writer or actor and shrivelling again into scenes of domestic life.

2

I did not wish for a theatre of despair, but I experienced despair. I wrote as a title, *Scenes of Overcoming*, thinking I might overcome

* Commissioned for an unpublished collection of essays. The title is the refrain of the clown McGroot from *The Power of the Dog*.

myself. I wrote also, *Choices in Reaction*, thinking of the choices I might myself have.

I always knew socialism was tragedy. I had represented it as tragedy early on, in *Fair Slaughter*. I had repeatedly studied its failure. But in the breaking of the politics of the time, I needed to know what meaning socialism had for me. I risked finding it had no meaning. It was no use repeating the catechisms. It was futile to rest a theatre on given things.

I found it possible to begin the play without socialism but to find socialism within the play. So the audience had to share my not knowing, when it was accustomed to being taught. I was in any case exhausted by certainty itself.

So the audience was sometimes angered, being used to the autocracy of the author, the Brechtian absolutism. I no longer wanted to tell the audience anything but to invite their participation in a hunting down of tolerance.

Consequently, I became less satirical, and satire had been one of my foundations, a skill I brought with me to the theatre, ready-made. But to be a satirist, you must know, and I knew less and less, not as an affectation (the conventional wisdom of diminishing knowledge) but through practical work in character.

The deterioration of habitual moral and political assumptions was the sole means by which a change in form became possible. This was inevitable at a time of political collapse. But the resistance had to lie in questions of first principle, which is the theatre's special territory. For example, our participation in acts of violence.

3

I wrote epic plays which commanded long entrances. I set my theatre in landscapes, not because I secretly wished to write film, but because the Polish swamp or the Flanders plain were manifestations of consciousness, just as the castle in *The Castle* is not set but the outcome of spiritual despair, and the burned out gaol in *The Hang of the Gaol* a massive shade of frustrated longing. But the Kremlin had to be implied by two plywood steps (*The Power of the Dog*) and the castle was shouted into place. Always the actor and the designer were flogged into substitution. This poverty of resource bore another corruption, which was to make it common belief the work was somehow remote, and the audience non-existent. The idea of the stable audience is a reactionary one, a blunt weapon used against the revolutionary text. It is a notion of the people used against people, and the sing-song of the populist state. The cultural managers will demonstrate the frivolity, the absence of concentration, the impatience, the dictatorship of television habits over the minds of the audience, but never the appetite for challenge, truth or discrimination. The Public, as an invention, becomes the enemy of the artist, a solid block of immovable entertainment-seekers whose numbers and subsequent economic power forbid intelligence. I refused this as a description of the audience and the description of myself as a problematical writer. I found, in collaboration with actors and directors, the audience for the work, sometimes half-hostile, but wanting. The tension between the audience and the play became for me an aesthetic, the nature of experience. This involved challenges to common morality, common socialism, even what passes for common humanity. So the theatre became for me a ground for assessment and potential reconstruction.

4

We make a fetish now of contradiction. We make banality of the discovery that the personal and the political do not sit, that socialism has violated as many as it has liberated, that the masses oppress as well as suffer, and that the individual is both an imperialist of the soul and the entire focus of freedom. And the contradictions pile upon each other in the Populist State. We find quality to be revolutionary, discrimination subversive, unanimity a spiritual poverty and the intelligentsia flinging its wits away, clambering through the decomposing heap of video and pop stars' bones that constitutes monetarist art. The surge of the Populist State, applauded by the left in one of its basest cultural spasms, medievalizes us, teaching us that literacy leads nowhere, that plague comes over the hill, from the Ukraine or Cumbria, and to fuck with strangers is to dice with death. All these contradictions we artistically rejoice in, finding it a sort of freedom, for the new man Brecht would have engineered is anathema to us, a mechanical proletarian cosmonaut, horribly unafraid. Our problem is to reach beyond contradiction, towards the ground of tragedy. If the legitimate incredulity which is our reaction to so much planned social disintegration is summed up in the refrain of Archie McGroot at the court of Joseph Stalin, 'Ye gotta laugh, no, ye gotta

[22]

laugh!' (*Power of the Dog*) then the task of serious art is to describe not wickedness but collusion, not simply authority but submission.

5

I gnawed at English socialism for ten years (from *Claw*, through *A Passion in Six Days*, to *Downchild*), coming at last to History, which is where I had begun, neither official history nor documentary history, whose truth I deny, but the history of emotion, looking for a politics of the emotions. I discovered that the only things worth describing now are things that do not happen, just as the only history plays worth writing concern themselves with what did not occur. New writing began at the Royal Court with the description of things that were not seen (i.e. real life). Writing now has to engage with what is not seen (i.e. the imagination) because real life is annexed, reproduced, soporific. The political play showed what is, but the reaction to what is has been only laughter, and through laughter, acquiescence. The political play must now return the onus to the audience, to the soul. A theatre which dares to return the audience to its soul, which has been seen by the left for so long as given, material, finite, oppressed, will experience the hostility a wrecked ship feels for the gale.

6

The individual must be denied the sanctuary of class.

The form of the play must reflect not its ability to report certain truths which at times cannot be told elsewhere, which renders it news, but its distinctive quality as form, which is the living actor, who cannot be confused with real life.

Everything is possessed except the imagination. We have laboured through a theatre whose naturalism has consigned imagination to the same dustbin as fantasy.

The task of theatre is not to produce cohesion or the myth of solidarity but to return the individual to himself. Not 'We must act!' but 'Are we thus?'

It is a simple task to persuade an audience of a character's evil. The important task is to persuade the audience of its potential or actual participation in evil.

A moral theatre is not one which separates the sheep from

negative empathy

[23]

the goats (the exploited, the exploiter) but accuses the exploited also.

Plays are much too short. The manager likes the short play, it fits his wage bills. The writer of short plays thinks 'they will grow impatient with me!' Because truth is complex, art is also complex. It cannot be smashed to fit the timetable of trains.

One day a play will be written for which men and women will miss a day's work.

It is likely this play will itself be experienced as work.

7

I came to theatre ignorant of almost every classic text and with half a dozen matinees behind me. I came to it because I could write speech and was impatient with novels, but also because it existed and clamoured for big and little texts, lunchtimes, studios, events. But for many years I could not justify my being there at all. I could not find any but the most instinctive motives for art of any kind. 'I had to . . .' 'I needed to . . .'. So self in motion seemed sufficient cause. But there seemed something shameful in using so public a medium for a private end, so I invoked my socialism, and talked of 'opposition', thinking I helped a class, or at best, was testament. Later, I found in the study of the artist himself (*No End of Blame*, *Scenes from an Execution*) the cause that was neither wholly self nor the rattling egotism of entertainment (which I also owned, but was suspicious of). This was a sense of artistic responsibility both to order and to violation, on the one hand to the language and the literary culture which was equipment only a fool tossed away, either out of wrong opposition or false solidarity with the uneducated, and on the other, to the furtherest reaches of speculation whether of desire or dissolution. I found the greatest moments in theatre were the most ambiguous, and truth, a thing we now hardly dare invoke, came only by excellence of the performer grinding on the complexity of text, and when it worked, worked against the will.

Conversation with a dead poet*

Middleton. You are an irresponsible optimist. You have deprived the audience of its right to moral satisfaction. Admittedly you have provided a violent conclusion, but with only one murder, when I wrote five or six. I do think this is an encouragement to bad morals.

Barker. What I have done is to insist on the redemptive power of desire, opposing your view on the inherent corruptibility of all sex. Livia is a much greater character than you allowed her to be. In any case, it is simply unrealistic to inflict slaughter on all the participants in the interests of morality. It was quite obvious to me you did not believe in that yourself but were fulfilling a convention.

Middleton. I wrote for an authoritarian Christian society. Authoritarian but not philistine. The King had just authorized a translation of the Bible. You inhabit an authoritarian society, but a philistine one. James the First did not think it silly to be an intellectual. He liked universities. I understand your government is closing them down. But yes, the ending is conventional. I had the censor to think of. Yet I believe the characters got what they deserved.

Barker. What attracted me to your play when Max Stafford-Clark, Artistic Director of the Royal Court, offered it to me was its obsessive linkage between money, power and sex. I saw the Florentine rulers as a rapacious class, vulgar and not very patrician. The Duke is characterized by cupidity.

Middleton. I knew very little of Florence. But we had to situate our politics at a distance. Otherwise you could end up in prison. How

---

* Published in *The Times*, 6 February 1986 under the title 'The redemptive power of desire', on the occasion of the performance of Barker's version of *Women Beware Women*.

do they punish you now? By taking the theatres away? It is much simpler.

Barker. England in this era is a money and squalor society, also. The connections were obvious. And money in your text corrupts everyone, though it appears to be sex that does it. I think you were only half-aware of this. Bianca is obviously seduced by the duke's wealth, not his body or his mind. And yet she immediately falls in love with him, the sexuality catching up with the acquisitiveness. The psychology of this is profound. It made me wonder what Bianca's sexuality consisted in. So I made her ask those questions, too, at a moment of terrible crisis. It launched my entire version. People start to ask, what is desire? What does it make me do?

Middleton. Your misfortune is that you have no notion of sin. Look how you have vandalized the Cardinal. You effectively remove the moral spokesman from my play, and replace him with a voyeur, a voyeur notwithstanding his intellectualism.

Barker. His speeches were conventional homilies for which a modern audience could have no sympathy. We still have writers who lecture the audience. Arguably a play is a lecture, but it must come at them obliquely, they are trained in suspicion. For us the question of the private morality of princes, or bankers, is not of the first importance, though it is hard to resist exposing it. The question for us is whether we should tolerate the deforming social effects of bankerdom itself. The sin of the false god. So I made Livia see that her life, most of which is behind her, had been rendered futile by her class affiliations. I always insist people can be saved.

Middleton. And I insist they are lost, that they have nothing but their instinct for survival. Leantio is my greatest character, a type new in my time, commonplace in yours. A middleman for merchants, he puts his love of his career even before passion. While he's absent on business, he loses his wife. Then he tries to lock her up like a piece of silver. That is a man! But, when he is robbed, he knows how to take the next opportunity. Money comes with a lecherous old woman, and he's bought!

Barker. You call Livia lecherous. She conceived an appalling desire, perhaps.

Middleton. It kills, her, anyway.

Barker. The solution to so much corruption can only be mass-murder, people falling down trap-doors and so on. It is as if you threw up your hands on human beings and wished them to hell.

Middleton. That is where they are bound for. And in case you condemn me as a cynic, remember it was I who wrote Leantio's 'Canst thou forget / The dear pains my love took, how it has watched / Whole nights together in all weathers for thee . . .?'

Barker. But it cannot endure. There is always perdition at the end of it.

Middleton. As night follows day.

Barker. Contemporary reactionary ethics would make such a viewpoint welcome. We are reviving a medieval social theology in which human nature is deemed incurably corrupt in order to reconcile the poor with poverty, the sick with sickness, and the whole race with extermination. Now also money is violent, but the torturer is the accountant. We require a different form of tragedy in which the audience is encouraged, not by facile optimism or useless reconciliation, but by the spectacle of extreme struggle and the affirmation of human creativity. Failure is unimportant, the attempt is all.

Middleton. This would explain your redemption of the low-life characters. Sordido in your version is a lout with a mission, and the Ward a study in pain. I think you are even more Christian than Shakespeare dared to be.

Barker. I did no more than lend them a status you suggested yourself.

Middleton. How?

Barker. By giving them so much wit. You could not resist giving them the gift of sarcasm. They are both wonderfully bitter at the expense of posturing women, and Sordido is the obvious ideal opponent for the Duke. I pushed the *nouveau riche* flavour of your Florence, its vulgarity and accompanying poverty, into a cultural

[27]

B

match for England now. Sordido is a model of modern youth, culturally embittered, a redundant genius who lives the life of the gutter. I massively extended the social range of your original by this one development.

Middleton. A final remark. How do you justify your continuing use of my title? What it means in my version is clear enough, but in yours?

Barker. In yours, a woman engineers the fall of a woman, for a man. That is the role of women in your time. In mine, a woman engineers the fall of a woman, but for her own enlightenment. But the pain is terrible. So the title finds an irony it never had in your play.

Middleton. May I congratulate you on assembling such a distinguished company of actors to perform this monstrous assault on the canon of English literature? It suggests to me that now, as in my time, the more ferocious the imagination, the more loyalty it commands.

On language in drama*

I would like to discard at the beginning of this paper any argument
about drama's responsibilities towards naturalism or what passes for
authentic speech. The defence of obscenity on the grounds that it is
prevalent in the street is not one which interests me or seems
specially legitimate. I have never been interested in reported speech
or the reproduction of authentic voices. Only those writers and
producers who claim to reflect life-as-it-is-lived are saddled with the
contradiction of deleting expletives and sexual nouns whilst claiming
to address people in their own tongue.

I would prefer rather to make a few points about the dramatist's
responsibility to a higher truth than mere authenticity. The drama
which I practise creates its own world, it does not require validation
from external sources, either of ideology or of spurious realism,
which is itself an ideology. It is compellingly imaginative and without
responsibility to historical or political convention. The audience is
made aware of this very rapidly – within a scene or two it is invited
to discard its normal assumptions about the manner in which reality
is reproduced. What is signalled is the appearance of different
dramatic values and what is witnessed is not the reiteration of
common knowledge but a dislocation of perceptions – in other
words, it is engaging with a work of art in which the normal criteria
of offence and empathy are abolished. I would stress that this is
nothing at all to do with entertainment, which is perfectly able to
operate within a limited vocabulary for the simple reason that it
operates within a limited range of emotions. A tragic drama exposes
the entire range of human emotions and attempts to extend it, and
it entails an obligation to explore, describe and speculate on all areas
of human experience. Language is the means by which emotion is

* Given as a paper at the BBC Seminar on Obscene Language on 14 June 1988 and
subsequently published in the *Independent* on 20 June 1988 under the title 'Irreplaceable
words'.

conveyed – in radio almost entirely so – and the two or three words we are so often exercised about are among the most highly charged in the vocabulary. Because of the responsibility of drama to emotional truth, these words cannot simply be abolished. The bland question so often put to writers, 'Do you really need those words?' rings with a false innocence. The hidden meaning of this question is 'Do you really need those feelings?' and attempts to restrict vocabulary are invariably attempts to restrict emotion. The words are irreplaceable for the reason that they are charged with a combined fear and longing. It is not for nothing that the word 'cunt' operates both as the most extreme notation of abuse and also the furtherest reach of desire, and not only in male speech, and in attempting to eliminate the word the thing itself is eliminated, since nothing can stand in for it. Since what cannot be expressed cannot exist dramatically, the attempt to abolish the word becomes an attack on the body itself – a veiled attempt to remove the body from dramatic space. The debate about words becomes a debate about the body, who owns it, and who describes it, and if the words are forbidden to the artist, the body reverts to the doctor. I would suggest that the aim of the language censor is to return the body to the biology class where eroticism is displaced and desire corrupted into a squalid fetishism. Furthermore, I would propose that those who seek to inhibit emotion in drama through the concept of obscenity betray a contempt for the audience. The false notion of a guardianship of values is in effect a bid for moral engineering.

I am a writer who has made and still does make conscious use of words conventionally described as obscene. I use them with calculation and discrimination for their dramatic effect. I place the words in the mouths of certain characters sometimes abusively, sometimes erotically, and sometimes with calculated excess, and always with the deliberate intention of creating the unease in the audience which is for me the condition of experiencing tragedy, an unease which is at the opposite pole from the apathy an audience feels in a state of entertainment. Drama, as I suggested above, is not life described but life imagined, it is possibility and not reproduction. The idea of obscenity is related to shame, and shame can be both employed and overcome by the fullest commitment of the actor and writer to the emotion described, to its validity and truth, and where this occurs the initial frisson of discomfort experienced by the audience in the presence of an actor arguing the body is replaced by an awe for the powers of human emotion. In this way the obscenity becomes a ground for moral revaluation.

Radical elitism in the theatre*

Most theatre managements, literary departments and directors would claim to be liberals, and class, gender, sexuality, violence, iconoclasm and blasphemy have all been welcome on their stages. There is only one sin left, and it is identified as elitism, a sin for which the left and right share an obsessive contempt, and consequently, it is a sin with compelling attractions. I would like to say a few things about sinning in the contemporary theatre, about sinners in art, and how I came to be one.

Like most fallen souls, I never meant it. I intended to be cruel, and witty, and in the old-fashioned sense, realistic . . . So I described what I knew, and after one short play, I had no more to add. I achieved a promising debut, but I sensed in the vaguest way I had not employed my imagination at all, I had merely reported on conditions. I was never to become a Royal Court writer. To articulate the profound dissatisfaction I felt took me a number of years. All I had to go on was a sense of opposition. I now know that what I wanted was a licence to speculate in a theatre that was resolutely naturalistic, and the courage to dream in a medium which had become reverential towards journalism and consequently, crucially documentary. This genre, of course, had its political gestation. In the post-war period identified around 1956, the bourgeois intellectuals who dominated and continue to dominate the theatre located not only the progressive, but also the sexual and the vigorous, in the working class, but being class-constructed themselves, took an essentially pessimistic view of the class's potentialities. Principally, they believed it lacked imagination. They wanted to know it, but only in forms they themselves constructed, principally, the theatrical form of naturalism . . .

To an extent 1950s naturalism and 1960s political theatre were

---

* Given as a paper at University of Cork, 21 November 1987, and subsequently published under the title 'The possibilities', *Plays and Players*, March 1988.

[32]

reactions against an effete and pseudo-poetical theatre which had surfaced after the war, a theatre whose anaemic rhythms and sham history made the thirst for an art closer to the life of 'ordinary people' more extreme. The headlong rush towards documentary theatre, which reached its apotheosis in the methods of the Joint Stock Theatre in the 1970s, sanctified research and the collective, emphasized 'relevance' as socially useful, and diminished the authorial identity. The writer remained the chief constructor of the play, but the onus was upon him to employ experience gained in collective work by the company, and the primacy of the message could not be concealed. The emphasis remained largely what it had been throughout the 1950s and 1960s – the exposure of living conditions, the exposure of capitalist rackets, the deprivation of classes. There is little ambiguity in the Royal Court play of the last 25 years, other than that surrounding the circumstances of its production.

In common with other writers I had made attempts on the naturalistic play by a number of means. Firstly, satire, secondly, in my case, by the effective banning of the room. There are rooms in my plays but they are peculiar rooms, rarely domestic and usually varieties of torture chambers . . . There are gymnasiums, banqueting halls, castles, burned-out gaols, but few domestic interiors. Unconsciously, I was resisting the reconciliation that the home enforces, for behind all domestic drama lies the spectre of reconciliation. Once the walls were taken down and the home abolished, imagination was liberated and speculation became possible. I was however, blocked from further progress by the very device which had initially released me from the naturalistic theatre: satire, The ease with which I could switch to a satirical mode is obvious from nearly any text. Tragedy, which was the only route, was effectively blocked by this recurrent impulse. A very good example of this is *The Power of the Dog*, which opens with a scene in which Churchill and Stalin divide the world, the Yalta meeting. So grotesque was the politics enacted at this moment in history that I could neither view it objectively nor discover a tragic form for it. The inescapable baseness of power broking on this scale commanded a satirical response, and it remains perhaps the finest satirical scene I have attempted, arguably dwarfing the anti-historical scenes that make up the bulk of the play . . . I would argue that it is not possible to destroy your enemies by comedy. The comedy that exists in my work is a cruel one, and the laughter that emerges uneasily from it is a laughter of disbelief and not a laugh of public unity . . . I realized that my theatre would be about dislocation and not unification. I knew the laugh I wanted would be strained and born of a profound confusion, or, as I wrote in the long poem *Don't Exaggerate* that Ian McDiarmid has so brilliantly performed, 'The irresistible collapse of words before the spectacle of unbidden truth'. I was wading into the heresy that would serve to isolate me from powerful elements in the English theatre . . .

The volume of massaging theatre produced by our major companies does not, peculiarly, indicate a lack of moral commitment. It is not a pure hunger for gold that has driven some of our best directors into the world of the musical. They may believe the conventional wisdom that art never changes anything, but in their hearts they are the tin crusaders of the new populism, with a positively renaissance appetite for personal gain on the one hand but a knocked-together ideology on the other. They think of an audience as something not to be trusted, as a semi-educated mass in need of protection, and protection in particular from complexity, ambiguity, and the potential disorder which lurks behind the imagination. With the end of full employment and the de-sanctification of welfare, the old liberal urge to please a morally confused and unhappy public by uniting it behind shallow collective responses became overwhelming. The conditions for the creation of Populist Theatre were all present when Thatcher took office. But the orchestration of populism was delegated to the liberal left who have, despite the apparently sweeping effects of political revolution, been left securely in office.

I must own up to the fact that even before I was identified as an artistic sinner conditions were never easy for my plays to find producers. I have described elsewhere the weary travels of my texts, and arguably the best ones suffered the longest. *Victory*, *The Castle*, *Crimes in Hot Countries*, *The Power of the Dog*, *The Love of a Good Man*, *Claw*, all waited years to find theatres. My major play on Helen of Troy, *The Bite of the Night*, has been abandoned by the Royal Court, who commissioned it, and has found no other home.* My play *The Europeans*, commissioned by the Royal Shakespeare Company, has been returned after a silence of nine months. The National Theatre has been offered every play of mine in the last ten years and ignored every one. And so on. I have been encouraged to join the actors Kenny Ireland and Hugh Fraser to set up a new

* Produced by the RSC at The Pit, August 1988, in a production by Danny Boyle.

[34]

company whose sole function is the production of Barker plays, The Wrestling School.*

A public has appeared for my theatre which does not appear to suffer offence in the way its guardians do, or more precisely, it is prepared to study its offence. In the midst of a surge in comedy and musical, a demand for intellectual intransigence has made itself apparent. This public appetite for the play of pain and problem made itself apparent during the season of my work at the RSC's Pit Theatre in 1985. The outstanding success of all the plays, but in particular of *The Castle*, a work of unremitting harshness conventionally described as pessimistic set in the crusades but entirely free of history, was almost certainly unexpected by the theatre management. When this season sold out, no attempt was made to extend the number of performances, nor has any plan to revive them ever been proposed . . .

It is a characteristic of this period, and one which again reminds us that nothing is what it was, and nothing will ever be what it was again, that a government of the extreme right – if that is what it is – should base its moral status on the idea of the infallibility of the People. . . . The manifestation of this inside the arts is a campaign against subsidy, and this is perfectly coherent, since if the People want your art they will obviously pay for it, and if they don't, by what right does it exist? Success here as in other fields is defined by financial return. Now this is the predictable programme of any right wing populist regime. What was unpredictable, however, was the extent of the collaboration in this exercise by proclaimed enemies of the right, who are the most vociferous in identifying the sin of elitism whether in the form of class-ownership of art forms, as in some opera, or in any art which might aspire to complexity, difficulty, or anything which has a literary tone, and I mean by that, the refusal of naturalistic speech and the elevation of language as the vehicle of complex articulation . . . It is the fate of words to pass from Heaven to Hell during the lifetime of a culture, but the degeneration of the word *elite* into an item of abuse has been more rapid than most. It stands in for anything that is not popularly and instantly comprehensible . . . .

Now there is nothing at all elitist about imagination, though few are as yet entitled to exercise it for a living. This is the privilege, but

---

* First production *The Last Supper*, March 1988, directed by Kenny Ireland.

also the responsibility of artists. An artist uses imagination to speculate about life as it is lived, and proposes, consciously or unconsciously, life as it might be lived. The more daringly he dreams, therefore, the more subversive he becomes. I have already talked about a theatre of journalism, and a journalists' theatre certainly isn't elitist. But neither is it subversive. No journalist ever suggested the possibility of other life, he can only expose existing life, and existing life, which has become raised into a cult – and a reactionary cult – in the phenomenon of the soap opera, forbids the imaginative.

A further easy-to-identify characteristic of the elitist theatre is its relative silence. You may have noticed that we live in a laughing society. The sound of laughter, mechanically reproduced, is the sound of this era. The status of comedians has never been higher. In my latest play, *The Last Supper*, laughter has become so artificial, so mechanical, that it has ceased to be attached to human beings at all, and drifts over the landscape like a storm cloud, discharging itself over battlefields and banquets alike . . . I would suggest that a theatre which takes itself seriously – and it must do if people are to take it seriously – cannot any longer afford to be comic. In a culture of diseased comedy, it can't laugh. Secondly, in an age of obsessive information, it can't afford to be factual. Facts we have in profusion, it is judgement we require. Thirdly, it must announce that life is complicated, and things are not what they seem. And fourthly, and this is why it is a radical theatre I am proposing, it must give the audience what it cannot any longer discover anywhere else – the honour of being taken seriously.

To take an audience seriously means making demands on it of a strenuous nature. There are people who wish to be stretched, challenged, even depressed by a work of art, and who will make considerable efforts to experience those things. The notion that concentration is shrivelling to forty-second spans has gained ground in a culture of kitsch television and advertising gimmickry. Boredom is produced by a failure to stimulate the imagination, and of course, kitsch is the enemy of imagination. Where imagination is stimulated, and the emotions engaged, concentration is possible for many hours. In my own theatre, great responsibility is borne by the actor in luring the audience into the unknown life that exists in the text – and here you have a moment of the purest, most radical elitism – the actor's skill, the writer's invention, together release the mind of the observer

[36]

from the blockage of unfreedom which is characterized in the feeling 'I don't know what this is about, therefore I reject it'. Instead the writer and the actor conspire to lure the mind into the unknown, the territory of possible changed perception . . . I believe in a society of increasingly restricted options that a creative mind owes it to his fellow human beings to stretch himself and them, to give others the right to be amazed, the right even to be taken to the limits of tolerance and to strain and test morality at its source.

Notes to *The Bite of the Night**

Social disfigurement finds no relief in the cosmetic of satire, which turns the object of scorn into an adored predator ('Oh, his energy, oh, his ruthlessness!').

The play for an age of fracture is itself fractured, and hard to hold, as a broken bottle is hard to hold. It is without a message. (Who trusts the message-giver any more?) But not without meaning. It is the audience who constructs the meaning. The audience experiences the play individually and not collectively. It is not led, but makes its own way through a play whose effects are cumulative. The restoration of dignity to the audience begins when the text and production accept ambiguity. If it is prepared, the audience will not struggle for permanent coherence, which is associated with the narrative of naturalism, but experience the play moment by moment, truth by truth, contradiction by contradiction. The breaking of false dramatic disciplines frees people into imagination.

Beauty, which in an era of cultivated philistinism is rare and secret, becomes a form of authentic resistance. In the theatre the restoration of beauty begins with the restoration of language.

The real end of drama in this period must be not the reproduction of reality, critical or otherwise (the traditional model of the Royal Court play, socialistic, voyeuristic), but speculation – not what is (now unbearably decadent) but what might be, what is *imaginable*. The subject then becomes not man-in-society, but knowledge itself, and the protagonist not the man-of-action (rebel or capitalist as source of pure energy) but the struggler with self. So in an era when sexuality is simultaneously cheap, domestic and soon-to-be-forbidden, desire becomes the field of inquiry most likely to stimulate a creative disorder.

The Bite of the Night is not contemporary, nor satirical, neither is

---

* First published as a programme note to a selective reading of the play, the Royal Court Theatre, 1987.

it short. It is mythical, tragic and very long. It is not a play of convenience, but full of demands, on tolerance and conscience. By the use of prologues and interludes it both reaffirms ancient traditions of theatre (a place of argument and ideological war within theatre itself) and ruptures the sequential, all-knowing character of most contemporary theatre. It expects no unity of response but encourages division, and restores responsibility to the audience. Thus to sense confusion is positive, and to laugh uneasily is to discover complexity, which is our greatest hope.

Prologues to *The Bite of the Night*

First prologue

They brought a woman from the street
And made her sit in the stalls
By threats
By bribes
By flattery
Obliging her to share a little of her life with actors

But I don't understand art

Sit still, they said

But I don't want to see sad things

Sit still, they said

And she listened to everything
Understanding some things
But not others
Laughing rarely, and always without knowing why
Sometimes suffering disgust
Sometimes thoroughly amazed
And in the light again said

If that's art I think it is hard work
It was beyond me
So much of it beyond my actual life

But something troubled her
Something gnawed her peace
And she came a second time, armoured with friends

Sit still, she said

And again, she listened to everything
This time understanding different things

This time untroubled that some things
Could not be understood
Laughing rarely but now without shame
Sometimes suffering disgust
Sometimes thoroughly amazed
And in the light again said

That is art, it is hard work

And one friend said, too hard for me
And the other said if you will
I will come again

Because I found it hard I felt honoured

Second prologue

It is not true that everyone wants to be
Entertained
Some want the pain of unknowing
Shh
Shh
Shh
The ecstasy of not knowing for once
The sheer suspension of not knowing
Shh
Shh
Shh
Three students in a smoke-filled room
Three girls on holiday
A pregnancy on a Saturday night
I knew that
I knew that
I already knew that

The marriage which was hardly
The socialist who wasn't
The American with the plague
I knew that
I knew that
I already knew that

We can go home now
Oh, car seat kiss my arse
We can go home now
Oh, underground upholstery
Caress my buttock
I loved that play it was so true
Take your skirt off
I loved that play it was so
Take your skirt off
What else are theatres for
Take your skirt off

This has to be the age for more musicals
Declares the manager
The people are depressed

This has to be the age for more musicals
Declares the careerist
Who thinks the tilted face is power
Who believes humming is believing

No
The problems are different
They are
They really are
I say this with all the circumspection
A brute can muster

I ask you
Hatred apart
Abuse apart
Boredom in abeyance
Politics in the cupboard
Anger in the drawer
Should we not

I know it's impossible but you still try

Not reach down beyond the known for once

I'll take you
I'll hold your throat
I will

And vomit I will tolerate
Over my shirt
Over my wrists
Your bile
Your juices
I'll be your guide
And whistler in the dark
Cougher over filthy words
And all known sentiments recycled for this house

Clarity
Meaning
Logic
And Consistency

None of it
None

I honour you too much
To paste you with what you already know so

Beyond the slums of England
Tower blocks floating on ponds of urine
Like the lighthouse on its bed of mercury

Beyond the screams of women fouled
Who have lost sight and sense of all desire

And grinning classes of male satirists
Beyond
The witty deconstruction of the literary myth
And individuals in the web of class
No ideology on the cheap
No ideology on the cheap

You think a thing repeated three times is a truth
You think to sing along is solidarity

No ideology on the cheap

Apologies
Old spasms
Apologies
Old temper

Apologies
Apologies

I charm you
Like the Viennese professor in the desert
Of America
My smile is a crack of pain
Like the exiled pianist in the tart's embrace
My worn fingers reach for your place
Efficiently

It's an obligation . . .

Honouring the audience*

Obviously, the English theatre is in crisis. Equally obviously, its crisis reflects the crisis in the liberal intelligentsia which owns the theatre. This crisis is an intellectual one. The question, 'What kind of theatre do we want?' is best answered from the point of view of 'What kind of audience do we want?' We are in fear of our own audience, as a poor teacher is afraid of the class.

The word which has seeped into the vocabulary is Celebration. We do not know what to celebrate however, if only because at certain times there is nothing to celebrate. The theatre we have created celebrates nothing, though it is usually filled with laughter. Laughter appears to be a manifestation of solidarity, but it is now more often a sign of subordination. It is pain that the audience needs to experience, and not contempt. We have a theatre of contempt masquerading as comedy.

The liberal theatre wants to give messages. It has always wanted to give messages, it is its way of handling conscience. But no one believes the messages, even while they applaud them. We are in a profound contradiction when the audience claps what it no longer honestly believes.

It is always the case that the audience is willing to know more, and to endure more, than the dramatist or producer trusts it with. The audience has been treated as a child even by the best theatres. It has been led to the meaning, as if truth were a lunch. The theatre is not a disseminator of truth but a provider of versions. Its statements are provisional. In a time when nothing is clear, the inflicting of clarity is a stale arrogance.

* First published in *City Limits*, 25 February 1988 under the title 'Honour thy audience'.

A new theatre will not be ashamed of its complexity or the absence of ideology. It will feel no obligations to lived life or to the journalistic impulse to expose conditions. It will not be about conditions at all. A theatre of conditions is a profoundly reactionary one, just as the insistently ideological is also reactionary. Like a party poster with its jabbing finger, it impels you to tear it from the wall. A new theatre will not force anyone to be free. Rather it will be an invitation to ask what freedom is.

A new theatre will put its faith in the will to knowledge, not knowledge given by the knowing, but the individual will to knowledge which is elicited by the experience of contradiction in the theatre. The dramatist explores the terrain, half-knowing, half-ignorant. His journey is mapped by the actors. The audience participate in the struggle to make sense of the journey, which becomes their journey also. Consequently, what is achieved by them is achieved individually and not collectively. There is no official interpretation.

A theatre which honours its audience will not therefore make an icon of clarity. If a scene might mean two things it should not be reduced to one. If a speech contains its opposite it should be played for its opposites. This is not to say a new theatre will 'see both sides of the question', which is impotence and stagnation. It will rather emphasize the essential instability of character and the untrustworthiness of opinion. We need a theatre of Anti-Parable, in which the moral is made by the audience and not by the actor. Naturally, this means the parable will be interpreted differently by different individuals. A good parable should provoke an argument and not a submissive nod of the head.

A theatre which honours its audience permits them to escape the nightmare of being entertained, to be left hungry, because theatre is not the providing of lunch. Until the theatre is seen as something other than a soup kitchen for the rich or a doss-house for the angry it will not be honoured in its turn, for the tramp is never grateful to the charity, any more than the plutocrat respects a waiter.

A theatre which honours its audience will demand of its writers that they write in hazard of their consciences, for writers are paid to think dangerously, they are the explorers of the imagination, the audience expects it of them. If they think safely, what is the virtue of them? Do you want to pay £10 to be told what you knew already? That is theft. Do you want to agree all the time? That is flattery, and the audience is always flattered, which is why it has become so sleek.

An honoured audience will quarrel with what it has seen, it will go home in a state of anger, not because it disapproves, but because it has been taken where it was reluctant to go. Thus morality is created in art, by exposure to pain and the illegitimate thought.

A new theatre will concede nothing to its audience, and the new audience will demand that nothing is conceded to it. It will demand the fullest expression of complexity, it will command the problem is exposed (but not solved). This new audience will demand more of the writers and the actor, and will itself set the pace of change. Only when the audience is insisting on change can the theatre be said to be in full flood. As things stand the audience is served, and its semi-conscious applause is deemed success. But genuine success is the point at which the audience, in a state of supreme seriousness, demands to be pulled further into the problem.

A new theatre will be over-ambitious. It will not settle for anything less than a full company of actors. The stage should swarm with life. No new writer should be taught economy, no matter what the economy demands. The new writer should be shown that the stage is a relentless space and never a room. If the new writer is taught economy the theatre will itself shrink to the size of an attic. It is probably time to shut the studio theatres in the interests of the theatre.

It was once believed that the writer who wrote for himself would end up speaking to himself. It was believed the writer had to write for others, i.e. using accepted practices of listening and seeing. But only the writer who truly invents for himself will acquire the audience who hungers for his invention.

The politics beyond the politics*

In an era of authoritarian government the best theatre might learn a different function. Abandoning entertainment to the mechanical and electronic, it might engage with conscience at the deepest level. To achieve this it would learn to discard the subtle counter-authoritarianism that lurks behind all satire, and cease its unacknowledged collaboration with the ruling order by not reproducing its stereotypes. It would unburden itself of an increasingly irrelevant didacticism and evolve new relationships with its audience which were themselves essentially non-authoritarian.

How might this be achieved? A first step might be the recognition that living in a society disciplined by moral imperatives of gross simplicity, complexity itself, ambiguity itself, is a political posture of profound strength. The play which makes demands of its audience, both of an emotional and an interpretive nature, becomes a source of freedom, necessarily hard won. The play which refuses the message, the lecture, the conscience-ridden exposé, but which insists upon the inventive and imaginative at every point, creates new tensions in a blandly entertainment-led culture.

The dramatist's obligation becomes an obligation not to a political position (the obvious necessity for socialism, etc., the obvious necessity for welfare, change, for kindness, etc.) but to his own imagination. His function becomes not to educate by his superior political knowledge, for who can trust that? but to lead into moral conflict by his superior imagination. He does not tailor his thought to an ideology, but allows it to range freely over a landscape in which he himself should experience insecurity, exposing his own morality, his own politics, to damage on the way. In an age of unitary thought and propaganda, this is his first responsibility. He forsakes in doing so his right to tell, he is destabilized, and this produces a critical attitude in his audience, which, since it is so bred into the doctrine

---

* Unpublished essay commissioned by the *Sunday Times*, 1988.

of messages, experiences at first the alienation felt by any public confronting a new art.

All this implies a tragic theatre. It implies the possibility of pessimism, which is wrongly associated by some with political reaction. It is a long time since my own theatre attempted acts of political instruction, though its satirical qualities always contained the hidden imperatives implicit in the form. *Victory* approached the problem of life in a post-liberal era by posing a series of accommodations, none of them respectable. Its pessimism was compensated for by its imaginative daring, its rupturing of moralities. *The Castle*'s interminable struggle between warped souls was never resolved – the play precisely lacked a politics of position – but its tragic scale, and the excoriation of feeling, lent to its audience a power to find confidence in catastrophe itself. In *The Possibilities* I recouped from a series of appalling situations a will to human dignity and complexity that came precisely from the absence of conventional politics. The unpredictability of the human soul, resistant to ideology and the tortures of logic, became a source of hope, even where death was inevitable. In *The Last Supper*, the longing for authority is shown to co-exist with a longing for its obliteration, and the play's determined refusal of the message created an uneasiness which was the sign of its relevance – neither catharsis nor epic. It is the authorial voice, straining to illuminate the blind, that prevents the proper focus of meaning in a work of art. The audience itself must be encouraged to discover meaning, and in so doing, begin some form of moral reconstruction if the politics of our time is not to become yet more narrow and intellectually repetitive. The left's insistent cry for celebration and optimism in art – sinister in its populist echo of the right – implies fixed continuity in the public, whereas morality needs to be tested and re-invented by successive generations.

The dramatist's function is now a selfish one. He must expose himself to tragic possibility by dragging into the light the half-conscious, the will to power, the will to negation, the ultimate areas of imagination which the conventional political play is not equipped to deal with. When the dramatist is himself heroic in the risks he is prepared to take with his material, his audience is honoured, and through a fog of early outrage, real changes of perception become possible. Plays of information ('how wonderfully researched!'), plays of communication ('we wish you to know the following!) are outflanked by a culture now obsessively concerned with dissemination of statistics and facts which themselves do nothing to stimulate change.

The artist's response to the primacy of fact must be to revive the concept of knowledge, which is a private acquisition of an audience thinking individually and not collectively, an audience isolated in darkness and stretched to the limits of tolerance. This knowledge, because it is forbidden by moral authoritarians of both political wings, becomes the material of a new drama which regards men and women as free, cognitive, and essentially autonomous, capable of witnessing pain without the compensation of political structures.

The consolations of ca

'Once, when I saw men with miserable faces star⌐   ⌐round, I
nutted them. In streets in Attica where I ran yobbish prior to the war, I
said cheer up you cunt and if they did not grin to order rammed my
forehead through their gristle. This was instinct but now I see it also must
be politics.'

The Bite of the Night, Act I

For some years I have been attempting to create a theatre which lent
its audience rights of interpretation. To do this has involved transgressing in the two sacred groves of contemporary theatre – Clarity
and Realism. The text or production which is lauded for its clarity
is inevitably the one which allows the least ambiguity, the least
contradiction, and the least room for evading the smothering sense
that someone is giving you a meaning to take away with you. It is a
form of oppression masquerading as enlightenment. Similarly, the
emphasis on Realism, now a term almost defunct but still plucked
like the last string of a battered guitar, presupposes a moral weakness
in the audience, which must be presented with positive landmarks,
like posts in an estuary, if it is not to be dangerously lost in the wastes
of imagination. These dominating critical categories are, however,
potent only so long as there is common ethical ground among artist,
actor and audience. As long as the moral landscape in which theatre
operated was morally coherent, whether Christian or Bourgeois-
Humanist, the artist's right to exhort, elucidate and educate was
unquestioned. The last decade has indicated such a deterioration of
the moral consensus that it is now reasonable to ask whether even
the most cherished statements of moral rectitude command a genuine
assent. For example, the voluntarist statement 'It is self-evident that
all men are created equal' does not, after a decade of Thatcherism
and the international retreat from Official Communism, carry the

* First published by *The Guardian*, 22 August 1988, under the title 'The triumph in
defeat'.

of authority that it once did. It requires examination, it to be reborn, and to be reborn, requires to be rediscovered. function of a theatre in this climate, whose laissez-faire coolness among men points to further fractures in social morality in spite of all propaganda to the contrary, must be to return the responsibility for moral argument to the audience itself. I believe this offers the artist new opportunities but also demands of him new practices.

I have suggested that in certain states of society it is better to take nothing for granted, and a crisis in public morality provides an aperture for a new kind of theatre which I believe must locate its creative tension not between characters and arguments on the stage but between the audience and the stage itself. This theatre intervenes at an earlier point in human relations than that at which it has done heretofore. The usual focus of contemporary theatre is how we live with one another on given moral predicates ('it is bad to hurt people', 'the unfortunate should induce feelings of pity', etc.), but clearly there is now a problem with the predicates themselves. A braver theatre asks the audience to test the validity of the categories it believes it lives by. In other words, it is not about life as it is lived at all, but about life as it might be lived, about the thought which is not licensed, and about the abolished unconscious. Sympathy, and the sudden liquidation of sympathy, the permanent disruption of character, the instability of motive, are some of the means available to this project. The abolition of routine distinctions between good and bad actions, the sense that good and evil co-exist within the same psyche, that freedom and kindness may not be compatible, that pity is both a poison and an erotic stimulant, that laughter might be as often oppressive as it is rarely liberating, all these constitute the territory of a new theatrical practice, which lends its audience the potential of a personal re-assessment in the light of dramatic action. The consequence of this is a modern form of tragedy which I would call Catastrophism.

The fallacy most warmly embraced by the entertainment industry in times of moral uncertainty is the one which insists depressed peoples hunger for song and oblivion. But as many hunger for the problem to be embraced as hunger for its abolition. A theatre of Catastrophe, like the tragic theatre, insists on the limits of tolerance as its territory. It inhabits the area of maximum risk, both to the imagination and invention of its author, and to the comfort of its audience. It commands the loyalty and attention of those for whom the raucous repetition of social platitudes of both left and right appear as aridities. But the conflict experienced between the audience and what it witnesses, its exposure to the unbidden thought, creates pain and even resentment. It is distinctly not an experience associated with entertainment, and consequently an audience needs to be both prepared and, as is the case with all new theatre, educated in its own freedom. Not being conducted either by fetishisms of Clarity or Realism, it must be liberated from its fear of obscurity and encouraged to welcome its moments of loss. These moments of loss involve the breaking of the narrative thread, the sudden suspension of the story, the interruption of the obliquely related interlude, and a number of devices designed to complicate and to overwhelm the audience's habitual method of seeing. The panic which can seize an audience, oppressed by years of trained obeisance, at 'losing the thread' (as if life were a thread), whether the author's (who since Brecht has been given the status of a deity in modern theatre, the one who knows all and is permanently in command of his thoughts) or the director's (who must impose coherence at all costs) must be replaced by a sense of security in not knowing, and welcoming the same risks the author himself took in charting unknown territory, and the actors took in making the journey with maps. As Adorno wrote of the great nineteenth-century novels, whose ambition the theatre must imitate if it is not to be made yet more tolerable and yet more brief, it derives its meaning precisely from the dissolution of coherent meaning.

The aim of a theatre of catastrophe in overwhelming the normal barriers of tolerance in its audience opens it to the complaint most frequently levelled at my work – the charge of pessimism. But pain and apparent defeat are not synonymous with pessimism, which is a narrow concept dear to the totalitarian mind and outlawed by the totalitarian state, where the idea of 'the depressing thought' as a threat to public morale has maimed literature and art. The nauseating cheerfulness of socialist realist literature, with its exhortations and beckonings to an impossible future, forced its practitioners to exercise their depression in private and contributed to the high suicide rate among 'progressive' artists. A similar imperative to enlighten, amuse, and stimulate good thoughts of a collective nature (family, nation, party, community) clings to the carnival mania of the left and the moral crusade of the right. But the banging of the drum is hollow and the rhetoric shallow. It is simply not credible. It is not the sum of experience. The catastrophe is also the property of the people, and it is the spectacle of human pain, of charismatic defeat, that constitutes the fascination and strength of tragedy. My own theatre has never aimed for solidarity, but to address the soul where it feels its difference. It is intended to plunge beneath the ground of common belief and to test the ground of first principles. The exhaustion felt by the audience in a theatre of this nature is not enervating, but the imagination is stimulated and the structures of morality are tested, even if only to be affirmed. But it is the audience who must calibrate and assess. Traditional tragedy was a restatement of public morality over the corpse of the transgressing protagonist – thus Brecht saw catharsis as essentially passive. But in a theatre of Catastrophe there is no restoration of certitudes, and in a sense more compelling and less manipulated than in the Epic theatre, it is the audience which is freed into authority. In a culture now so rampantly populist that the cultural distinctions of right and left have evaporated, the public have a right of access to a theatre which is neither brief nor relentlessly uplifting, but which insists on complexity and pain, and the beauty that can only be created from the spectacle of pain. In Catastrophe, whose imaginative ambition exposes the reactionary content in the miserabilism of everyday life, lies the possibility of reconstruction.

Beauty and terror in the Theatre of Catastrophe*

I want to discuss the idea of beauty and its political implications in some of my plays. It seems to me there are moments of graphic beauty in the staging of certain scenes and an accompanying beauty of expression, which, despite the terror of the event described, or because of it, complicate and subvert the ostensible meaning. I believe this reflex in what might be called my writing personality accounts for the density of the experience and the impossibility of reducing it to fixed interpretations. I take it for granted, of course, that the play is not a lecture and therefore owes no duty of lucidity or total coherence.

I would like to take as a first example the final scene of an early play, *Claw*, which was first performed at Charles Marowitz's now defunct Open Space Theatre in 1975, and was my first three-act play. I regarded this play at the time as a didactic play of politics demonstrating false consciousness, the futility of individualism and the myth of social mobility. The protagonist, an illegitimate war baby, defying his stepfather's gnawing insistence on class-solidarity, succeeds brilliantly in his chosen career as a pimp. His activities place him in conflict with a government minister whom he numbers among his clients. He threatens to expose the man's private scandal, and, misjudging his own power, finds himself incarcerated in the wing of a mental hospital which is effectively a death-chamber. Alone with his two warders, one a former assistant to the now redundant hangman, the other a turned IRA man, he senses the imminence of his death and the absolute eradication of any trace of his existence. As a single individual, he faces obliteration for the arrogance of his challenge to organized authority. In his extremity, he appeals to the spirit of his stepfather, the monotonous reciter of Marxist texts, now dead or dying in a home for the aged. The ghost appears, and exhorts

* Given as a paper at the Day School on Howard Barker, Birkbeck College, London, 10 December 1988.

[55]

him to make passionate appeal to his gaolers on the ground of their common class origin, their unarticulated proletarian solidarity, and their essential frailty in a world of brute power and manipulative politics. This speech, which is at the same time a biographical adieu, sets a tone of poetry and pity which makes a painful contrast with the environment of the death cell. Now, in a supreme effort of articulation and imagination, the redeemed pimp appeals to his killers, who hear him out with a proper consideration. The pimp completes his prayer, and in a state of exhaustion, awaits their verdict. This silence is, I suggest, the supremely beautiful moment of a play which is a journey through the stagnant pool of unlived life, soiled feeling and the moral destruction of both poverty and privilege. It is also the political climax, since it proposes to the audience the possibility of celebration, redemption and revival. As in all my plays, the antipathy felt by the audience towards an unattractive protagonist has been eroded by an intimacy of feeling accumulated over a long evening – the audience wills survival on the victim. It also wills the endorsement of the political posture of the despised parent. And it finally wills the dramatic optimism usually associated with survival. But the speech fails. The warders reach for the concealed bathtub which is to be the instrument of the hero's death. He is drowned, without resistance, on the stage. Thus the optimistic possibility is exploded – if optimism it is – and didacticism is scattered in a surge of terror.

I would suggest that, despite its relative earliness as a play, this scene in *Claw* is typical of a method which characterizes my approach to the idea of political meaning. In the first place, the galloping threat of a message is annihilated by the intervention of a superior claim – that of dramatic beauty, in the same way as the potential slogan is always suffocated by the complex beauty of language delivered of its naturalistic bondage. Secondly, the visual beauty of the moment of the appeal made by the victim – his position mid-stage between two white-coated figures whose casual brutality we have at some length become acquainted with – saturates the context in which didacticism thrives. The objectification of the moment is thwarted by a complexity of emotions. Lastly, the speech itself, passionate but above all linguistically remote from common speech, even if littered with references, removes it from the realist mode. The failure of this speech, signalized not by any verbal response, but by the simple action of one of the murderers in switching on a transistor radio, is overwhelming in its horror and, assuredly, in its inevitability. In one sense, the moment confirms the worst fears of the audience, that people cannot be changed, that pity is rare, that passion is always drowned in expediency. But I would now like to suggest that the context of the scene, which is one of beauty and terror, provides a political subversion of a more complex kind than the didactic form that the play at first appeared to favour. In effect, the play subverts itself, the conclusion, in its failure to project the message, obliging the audience to digest the experience in an individual way, but the beauty of the scene forbidding its extinction in the memory. The frustration of the message sets up an anxiety, while the beauty of the scene locks it in the imagination.

Claw is an early example of what I later formulated as a drama of Catastrophe, but lacking the element of conquest which appears in the later plays. In other words, the protagonist does not reconstruct himself out of his circumstances. Claw, the name he elects for himself, is symbolic of violence, but never of discovery, and though he travels the breadth of society, he does not journey within himself.

In more recent plays, the substitution of beauty and terror for explicit political statement, the rejection of the expected line on a given subject, create those tensions in the audience that characterize the Catastrophic play. Tension is derived from the contradictory currents felt when wrong actions are passionately performed in pursuit of self-consciousness. I would like to take an example from my 1983 play, *Victory*, set during the restoration of 1660 and performed by the Joint Stock Company under Danny Boyle. The protagonist Bradshaw, widow of a republican intellectual, chooses to expose herself to the full blast of circumstances by abandoning her home, and, in gathering the dismembered parts of her husband's body, live a life of suspended morality. The act of collecting her husband together, futile as she discovers only in the final scene, is itself an act of extreme piety, but in doing so she consciously destroys in herself the moral habits of a lifetime. She creates a character better suited to the changed politics of the state. After months of criminal and vagrant existence, she arrives as a refugee in the London garden where Milton, the last representative of passionate republicanism, is being sheltered by a reactionary royalist. That is simply the first contradiction of the scene. The poet has been an intimate collaborator of Bradshaw's dead husband, and there is every reason to expect the two victims of the reactionary vendetta to throw themselves together and console themselves for disaster. But Bradshaw has banned this kind of reconciliation from her life. The spectacle of the blind Milton fills her with contempt, and in a surge of cruelty and mischief she strikes him across the face, deriding him. In this scene, which exemplifies the collapse of solidarity and the suspension of morality, the beauty of Bradshaw's exhilaration, her poetic recollection of lost and unrecoverable life, combined with her terroristic attack on a helpless man, serve to create a dramatic climate where political values are loosed into the air, and the audience, deprived of the predictable, is obliged to construct meaning for itself, at least until the stricken Milton, nursing his smacked face, settles the chaos in a moving but essentially trite revolutionary catechism.

The removal of the moral climate from a scene – or, more precisely, the suspension of moral predictability – reaches a sort of apotheosis in my work in the ten short plays called *The Possibilities*, which were seen at the Almeida in 1988 in a production by Ian McDiarmid. Each of the plays predicates a politics of oppression. In the various circumstances of the plays, historic, contemporary, theocratic or collectivist, the characters are invited to behave diplomatically, logically or expediently by superior powers. In the one play I wish to discuss here, called *Kiss My Hands*, the wife of a radical activist inadvertently betrays her husband to his murderers, who visit their home at night. She allows them entry when they plead they have a sick comrade with them. Her husband has already thoroughly rehearsed her in the rules of not opening doors, and her lapse leads to his murder. As he is dragged away to be shot, she experiences a fit of remorse and horror, and calling her child from his bedroom, she attempts to suffocate him with a pillow, staggering over the stage in a breathless struggle whose intention is to prevent the world inflicting any further damage on his innocence. Like the moment of Bradshaw's attack on Milton, this action, in its choreography and its complete surprise, is dramatically beautiful and intellectually subversive, its power deriving from what is, objectively speaking, wrong thinking. After an almost intolerable duration, the woman abandons her attempt at infanticide, recovers some degree of mental stability, and embracing her child, declares, in what must be a supreme burst of contradictory logic, that she will continue to open the door. Objectively therefore, she may be considered to be insane, since opening the door was precisely the cause of her pain. This play, like the others, offers neither advice nor instruction. It is ideologically void, and like the other two examples I have suggested, cannot be comprehended in the normal terms of political discourse. None of the three examples I have described is suggestive, nor are they manipulative of the audience in a 'realist' way, since they do not aspire to indicate 'correct' action, or 'correct' analysis. Furthermore, in their complexity and contradictory nature, they divide the audience into its individual components, a moment of fragmentation that I believe to be a significant characteristic of a theatre of Catastrophe. This return to individual pain is unassuageable through recourse to political orthodoxy, but the power of its visual and linguistic poetry enhances the nature of the problem to an extent that denies the possibility of catharsis and creates a genuine moral anxiety. In this way, catastrophic beauty is in my view more deeply subversive than critical realism purports to be.

If a theatre of Catastrophe takes as its material the individual and the individual's ability to effect self-identification in a collective or historical nightmare, the moment of beauty is the moment of collision between two wills, the will of the irrational protagonist (the non-ideological) and the will of the irrational state (the officially ideological). In my most recent play, *The Europeans*, commissioned by the RSC but deemed unsuitable for its public, the maimed casualty of a war between empires makes public her atrocity in an attempt to prevent her pain becoming subsumed in the anodyne reconciliations which pass for public history. Refusing to permit her biography to degenerate into a statistic, she delivers the child which is one of the products of her ordeal, in a public place, struggling even against the midwives to establish the primacy of her experience over the public interest. This scene, which contains all the elements which constitute beauty and terror, is deeply unsettling, but not for the obvious reason that childbirth is rarely enacted on the stage – rather, the catastrophic enterprise of the heroine at her most assertive and irrational exposes the false content of the values that are being imposed on her, and reveals pity, reconciliation and forgetfulness as instruments of political oppression, the annihilation of individual pain in collective orthodoxy. The crucial characteristic of this, as in the other examples I have given, is that the moment of beauty is also a moment of 'wrong action'. It is precisely its 'wrongness' that is the source of its disturbance. The anxiety that is experienced as a social faux pas is here enlarged into a dramatic form, but the initially offensive nature of the action is rapidly revealed to have its own

[59]

C

justifications in the struggle of the character to achieve some self-identification: the mother wrongly trying to suffocate her child, the tramp wrongly attacking the poet, the wilful obscenity of giving birth in the gutter. The audience, forced to re-view, re-feel, a 'wrong' action, is provoked and alerted, and launched unwillingly into consideration of morality, rather than subdued by the false solidarities of critical realism.

Juha Malmivaara's *Scenes from an Execution*, Turku, Finland, 1988

Malmivaara had failed with *The Love of a Good Man*, despite the power of his production. The audience had deserted him, walking out of the theatre. When I went to receive my bouquet, I looked out into emptiness. Malmivaara needed to prove the necessity for Barker.

He made a significant discovery. He understood that with Barker the theatre itself was a barrier to communication. He recognized that the structure of the building and its status in the community were injurious to the power of the work. The theatre-as-monument infected the audience, excluding whole groups of the community and reinforcing the commoditization of art.

He chose, instead of allowing the audience to sit in judgement on the work from the jury box of the stalls, to insist on their discomfort, which was the same discomfort experienced by the actors. He made the audience pay a price for its art by placing the production in a mile-long shed. When they saw this shed, the audience knew the conditions were different. They were prepared for the play to be different, and were obliged to suspend their instincts of judgement as well as their demands for pleasure. They knew they had forfeited their rights over the actors, and instead felt privileged to witness them. It was the actors who commanded them to see, and they crowded round each other to see better, breaking the conventions of normal witnessing. It was they who made adjustments. It was they who came as innocents to the imaginative world. Malmivaara insisted they came to art in this way, disarmed.

In one scene he placed the audience in prison with the actor. In pure darkness he obliged them to experience at least one aspect of incarceration. Then, from a distance of hundreds of yards, the light of a lantern came. The relief of this light was a metaphor for hope. The audience trusted Malmivaara, whilst being uncertain what he would do with them next. This tension was the best condition for viewing the plays of Barker.

He knew the importance of difficulty in art and the repulsiveness of easy art. The difficulty of the text he counterpointed in the difficulty of the situation. But he did not fail to reward the audience. He gave them, above all, beauty. For their effort he rewarded them with things they had never seen before, just as the text insisted on things that had not been exposed before. He knew in theatre each production must give what cannot be reproduced in any other medium. So when the drunken sailors entered Galactia's studio, they careered from a vast distance, and their mayhem was a thing of beauty, in its music and its choreography. The audience knew this could never be witnessed again. They felt privileged. In an ordinary theatre they would have thought such things merely their due.

Malmivaara showed by this production the sacrifices audiences will make for art, the pain they are willing to share with the performers. He did not give them the simple gratifications of community theatre, with its known virtues and facile ends, but led them into deeper and deeper complexity by relieving them of the burden of prior knowledge, the burden of authority which is a barrier to new experience. He took control from them, and gave it to the actors. They dominated the audience, who were not raked above them like delegates.

Malmivaara understood that in the Barker play the audience must suspend its critical faculties and swallow the passing offence. It must give itself into the hands of the actors and delay its judgement while the play completes its journey. To achieve this he perfected a fluidity between scenes which overlaid each other, drawing the attention from place to place and emotion to emotion. He gave them no time to digest the experience, making the journey of the play a literal one. In this he approximated to the text itself, which is a river of words and images. In the static theatre the audience is gnawed by its lack of control. In Malmivaara's sheds the audience was propelled by the pace of the action and could not dwell on what it had experienced. The fatal inertia induced by the surroundings of the conventional theatre was therefore prohibited.

On Nigel Terry's performance of Savage, in *The Bite of the Night**

Terry welcomed the opportunity to forfeit his own glamour. He had played so many attractive men. He had been the essence of the Romantic actor. He had played Caravaggio, Charles II, Byron, King Arthur. Now he played an unhealthy fat man whose movements were essentially comic. Terry had reached a point in his life when his profoundly curious imagination led him beyond self-consciousness, and at this moment a text appeared which was a means to his growth as a performer.

Terry experienced the journey in each performance, as any good actor must. But he found in Savage the innocence which is a crucial ingredient in evil and so brought us to fresh understanding. He saw that evil was small in its origins, and begins with insignificant mischief, even in wit. He saw that it was childish. Thus he made his audience party to his ebullience. He charmed his audience with his absurdity and was not afraid of losing face, so that his cruelty came harder on the nerves, and wounded more.

He cavorted in his moments of triumph, converting his intellectual satisfactions into physical action. In that cavorting was contained the essence of evil will. By this he demonstrated the actor's choice of significant physical expression making manifest internal states. But he did not hang his performance on the hook of his gestures. He was not corrupted by his invention. He had studied the lightness of the fat man, who is neither lethargic nor clumsy, but often dances on the tips of his toes. In this lightness he reached through time to the worst of the Caesars.

He found a posture in which to watch the unforgivable act. In this posture he conveyed the combination of horror and curiosity that attends all of us in the presence of pain. Eventually, this posture developed an ease, a casualness, an objectivity, which was the essence of his corruption. In the beginning he suffered the horror of parting

* RSC Pit Theatre, 1988.

with sympathy, and at the end, he bathed in his own indifference. Thus in this figuring of the body, he revealed the labour of his journey.

Often in rehearsal he cried out 'I don't know what I'm doing!' Angrily, he contended with the most complex motivations which were not always explicit in the text. He found these by excavating himself, by going deeper into self than actors are required to go. In the risks he took with his own conscience, he enabled the audience to forgo the usual satisfactions of identification without forcing alienation upon them. He implicated them in his acts, unsettling the routine relations of actor and audience. He insisted on the humanity in inhumanity.

He controlled the language without being controlled by it. He did not allow even the moments of rhetoric to lose their thread to the character. Instead he showed the character Savage employing rhetoric as part of his own creative and imaginative world. It was not the actor Terry who became rhetorical but the character Savage indulging his rhetorical skills. But beyond this, he revealed under the performance of the rhetorician the character's will, his pain, or fear, which he demonstrated was often at variance with the content of the speech. None of this was too complex for him.

On watching a performance
by life prisoners*

In the performance they affirmed the drama as freedom. They asserted the superior life of the imagination. In the moment of performance they were not in custody.

They created character from a longing for other life. They demonstrated by their conviction that drama was a necessity and not a pleasure or a diversion.

They had committed terrible acts, which made them objects of curiosity for their audience, who were not criminals. But they obliterated their reputations by their authentic portrayal of character. They shouldered away curiosity by the power of their concentration, and made the text more fascinating than their false glamour. Their concentration was greater than the concentration of professional actors, who do not bring bad reputation with them. They outplayed the voyeur.

They had no fear of the text. They were of mixed intelligence, and little education. But they showed no humility towards language or poetry. Though they had been crushed by life, and had crushed it, they responded to the power of articulation in the text which they themselves could not achieve. They felt gratitude for the existence of speech and metaphor, and made it their own, though it was not the language of the gaol. For all their appalling experience, they ached for the deeper experience of imagination.

They did not want to act what they already knew. They had no sentiment for the naturalistic mode. They wished to inhabit other life, and felt sympathy for pain in types they had never encountered, or situations they had not dreamed. In this the gaol was overcome, even while the guard dogs barked in the yard below.

In a place which licensed no pity, they found it possible to express pity. They guarded this closely, as a privilege. They shielded it from the observation of others, who would have derided it, and exposed

* *The Love of a Good Man*, Wormwood Scrubs, 7 July 1988, directed by Alan Cormack.

[65]

it only in the room which was called a theatre. So I learned that theatre was a place where feeling was permitted which was denied elsewhere.

They took the text to their cells and for months pored over it. In working the text they allowed the forbidden faculties to breathe, so that their performance was made both as actor but also as audience. In this they were unlike professional actors – the play was a substitute for lived life.

At the end of the performance they were locked in their cells, so the possibility of collective satisfaction was denied them. Alongside this play other prisoners performed a light comedy. These prisoners were not allowed to see the play. It was considered by the authorities that the bulk of the prisoners would object to the play. They would disrupt the production and might attack the actors. In a prison, the active power of morality, its coercive intolerance, is expressed most violently. The criminals, for all their bad acts, would not tolerate transgression. The gaol was thus a society as tightly regulated as the outside by relativist morality. In this society, microcosmically, theatre was perceived as an affront. What nourished some was abominated by others.

The offer, the reward,
and the need to disappoint

In the old theatre, the actors offered the play as a salesman displays his product – unctuously and with fake gentility. The prologue was the patter of the potentially unemployed. Thus the audience became customers, whose satisfaction was the necessary end of the performance.

In the new theatre, the audience will offer itself to the actors. It will relinquish its status as customer and abandon its expectation of reward. When it ceases to see itself as customer, it will also cease to experience offence.

The reward is a relic of the market place. The old theatre pretends to reward its audience for its effort of attendance, its effort at concentration, its surrender of futile time. You must reward the audience, say the poor critics. Why? Is theatre so intolerable? Is art not necessary for itself? The contrary is the case. It is a privilege to witness art. It is a privilege to hear good actors. In the new theatre there will be no reward because there will be no deal, no swop, or compact. The new theatre will not perceive itself as product. The audience will enter the new theatre out of necessity. In this condition, which is the compulsion of a spiritual hunger, it will cease to pass facile judgements on the play.

To escape the pernicious memory of the market place, the new theatre will dethrone its audience. The audience will no longer sit in tiers. It will not be encouraged to think itself a jury, obsessively judgemental. The actor will dominate the audience, not only by his performance, but also by his elevation above the audience. The audience is not to be rendered uncomfortable, nor attacked. We are not seeking a theatre of masochism. But it must be delivered from the shallowness of its expectations, its appetite for rewards. This narcissistic frisson is a relic of the exchange-relation, and of cultural infancy.

The infantile notion of the reward, which still dominates the serious theatre, is based on critical clichés. The audience feels the reward if it senses the play's 'importance'. Infantile critics are forever in search of 'important' plays. The important play cannot exist, however, without denying its own importance. This is because to be recognized as such it must trade in the very cultural, political and social conventions that constitute the discourse of the world *outside* the theatre. In other words, it replaces, reorganizes, or re-perceives the elements of existent ideology. It could not avoid or demolish these without sacrificing its 'importance'. The play that fails the test of 'importance' is invariably felt to be disappointing. The Disappointing play refuses to gratify the audience's thirst for social and political repetition. It robs its audience of the grotesque satisfaction of identifying its enemies and celebrating its prior knowledge – the sickening and secret compact between the author and his audience that distinguishes liberal art.

The Disappointing play squirms away from the notion of 'importance', and instead of offering the reward, delivers the wound. The wound is the aim of the new theatre and the intention of the actor. His performance will create the wound and the wound will be the subject of continuing anxiety. Only anxiety will justify the efforts of the performance. This anxiety will come from the audience's attempt to experience the play outside the confines of ideology. Slowly, the audience will discover the new theatre to be a necessity for its moral and emotional survival. It will endure the wound as a man drawn from a swamp endures the pain of the rope.

The audience, the soul, and the stage

When did you last hear a laugh which was
Not a spasm of intoxication
Not a gesture of solidarity
Not a gurgle of vanity
The choral assent of intellectual poseurs but
The irresistible collapse of words
Before the spectacle of truth?

I never have

(*Don't Exaggerate*)

To discuss the practical or theoretical nature of a contemporary theatre it is necessary to begin from the state of public knowledge. Only from a judgement regarding the state of public knowledge, its sickness or its vitality, can the necessary forms of theatre be deduced.

The Theatre of Catastrophe takes its form from the following assessment:

That information is a universal commodity

That knowledge is forbidden

That imagination has been maimed by collectivist culture

That in this maiming the public itself has colluded

But that this collusion is nevertheless detected and is experienced as shame

The Theatre of Catastrophe addresses itself to those who suffer the maiming of the imagination. All mechanical art, all ideological art, (the entertaining, the informative) intensifies the pain but simultaneously heightens the unarticulated desire for the restitution of moral speculation, which is the business of theatre. The Theatre of Catastrophe is therefore a theatre for the offended. It has no dialogue with

Those who make poles of narrative and character

Those who proclaim clarity and responsibility

Those who ache to delight the audience

Those who think laughter is a weapon of the oppressed

Those who dream theatre tells the truth

Those who insist on the facts

Those who clamour for fantasy

Those who believe in the existence of ordinary people

The Theatre of Catastrophe is rooted in the idea of the soul, not as immortal form, not as a thing immune from damage, but as innate knowledge of other life. In some, this knowledge is nothing more than a cherished hoard of stereotypes (the sea, the sky, the prospect of love). In others, the Soul breaks with all images it senses corrupt or annexed by ideology (harmony, family, the public) and aspires to new forms. The Theatre of Catastrophe addresses those imperatives of the Soul which most writhe under reproduction. It exhilarates. It creates offence, even among the already offended. It does not limit its address to the educated, though it does not honour ignorance. Above all, it speaks a new language, which is to say it believes language to be revolutionary in a culture which degrades language and smears it as elitist. It makes language as luscious and as spiteful as love, of which it is an expression. It abhors reconciliation which is not won at terrible cost. It demands more of its audience than all existing theatre.

The audience of this theatre is in awe of the actor. It is in awe of him because the actor does not pretend to be the audience (a theatre of recognition) but asserts his difference. He both suffers more, and exposes more, than the audience anticipates. The audience of the Theatre of Catastrophe is not gratified to see its life reflected on the stage. It comes with a single desire – to witness unlived life, which the ideological and the mechanical conspire to conceal. In this, the Theatre of Catastrophe is more painful than tragedy, since tragedy consoles with restoration, the reassertion of existing moral values. The audience is not flattered with hope, but rather lent pain. It is not taught criticism, but honoured with the truth of the absence of truth. It leaves the theatre privileged, but unrewarded. It does not cluck with collective satisfaction, but divided and solitary, it labours with the burden of an art that denies assimilation.

The humanist theatre*

We all really agree.
When we laugh we are together.
Art must be understood.
Wit greases the message.
The actor is a man/woman not
unlike the author.
The production must be clear.

We celebrate our unity.
The critic is already
on our side.
The message is important.
The audience is educated
and goes home
happy
or
fortified.

The catastrophic theatre

We only sometimes agree.
Laughter conceals fear.
Art is a problem of understanding.
There is no message.
The actor is different in kind.

The audience cannot grasp
everything; nor did the author.
We quarrel to love.
The critic must suffer like
everyone else.
The play is important.
The audience is divided
and goes home
disturbed
or
amazed.

* First published in *Théâtre en Europe*, 1989.

Theatre without a conscience*

There is a type of theatre which has dominated us for the last two or three decades which takes as its starting point, its inspiration, even, the apparently selfless desire to make people better. It is the kind of theatre which begins, long before the process of writing or rehearsal, with the question, 'What do people need?' When this need has been identified, the search for a subject begins. The insatiable appetite for improving other people can be detected in the way in which writers and directors justify and advertise their efforts. If a writer is asked why he wrote a particular play he or she invariably replies 'I wanted people to understand such and such a thing better', or 'I wanted people to know how such and such a person feels', or 'I wanted to heighten their perception of such and such an issue', and even, at its most shamelessly ambitious, 'I wanted to improve the quality of people's lives.' In all these responses there is a passion to enlighten, a paternalistic beneficence, from the one who knows to the many who do not, the largesse of perception dished out in the palaver of dramatic form. This is the social hygiene of the gifted aching to illuminate the ungifted, the above-prejudice correcting the prejudiced, and the artist instructing the herd. It is the essential manner of the humanist play, which has as its project the strictly utilitarian end of making us good and happy (happiness supposed to be derived from 'understanding one another') and turning theatre into sticking plaster for the wounds of social alienation. This is the theatre of daylight, clarity and dubious truths, behind which lies the critical consensus that art is somehow to do with 'informing'. Who hasn't read again and again the satisfied reviewer announcing in these terms why he had a good night out – 'I left the theatre knowing more about this subject than when I went in . . .', 'I was enlightened about . . .', 'The play made me realize', etc., the clucking of customers who have got their fistful of knowledge, the sort of accolade that is the

* Given as a paper at the University College of Wales, Aberystwyth, 6 October 1990.

[72]

erosion of theatre as art and the triumph of a theatre of social correction. And of course, because the desire to correct and be corrected is an irrepressible human drive, the demand for such a theatre is continuous. We have had for some decades now the spectacle of dramatists who haunt the newspapers for their inspiration, indeed are wholly dependent on it, as well as theatre companies of some distinction whose most significant activity is what they call 'researching material', an activity closely related to the business of 'dramatizing' things. Theatre has no business with research, and things are not dramatized: they are either drama or they are something else. They come into existence as art, or they are not art at all, and research is something carried out by specialists called academics or non-specialists called journalists. The verb 'to dramatize' is part of the kitsch vocabulary of the theatre of issues, in which actors are employed as a means to a didactic end, the education of the ignorant audience, and by 'research' we are threatened with the spurious legitimacy of so-called facts. 'It's all right', the actors seem to tell you in researched plays, 'everything we demonstrate has occurred', is in effect 'true'. But the theatre is not true, it is not a true action, its very power, its whole authority comes from the fact that it is not true, and the idea of accuracy, or reference to a source outside the theatre walls, is fatal to its particular unsettling and revolutionary power. The moment that an action on the stage asserts its veracity by reference to known and proven action elsewhere, theatre is overwhelmed by the world, the world reclaims it. It is a symptom of the lost faith in theatre as an art form that its practitioners require the credentials of authenticity. It is the poverty of the journalist that he must provide evidence for his assertions, the frailty of the academic that he must prove and counter-prove. The theatre is without evidence, it 'makes believe', it forces belief. The audience of the theatre comes for what it cannot obtain elsewhere in any other forum. In other words, it comes for the false, it comes for the speculative and the unproven. The researched theatre says, the informative theatre says, 'we have demonstrated such and such a fact, and it will make you better to know it', a sham democracy behind which lies a repugnant arrogance. The imaginative theatre says 'we prove nothing, we assert that nothing can be proved by the actor'.

Let us not pretend, however, that the Theatre of Conscience does not have its attractions in the contemporary world. There is an obvious base pleasure to be had in enlightenment of this kind, a gratifying trade-off between customer and performer. You pay £5 or £10 for a seat and you are sent home with an item of sympathy or knowledge, you grasp what you are intended to grasp, some facts about a researched subject, some insight into the social conditions of somebody, you are officially encouraged to extend sympathy to a chosen group of fellow human beings, which is easily done in art if not in life, and your conscience is effectively massaged. If a theatre of entertainment is a deal, so is the theatre of enlightenment. As the writer says in his interview, 'I wanted people to understand such and such a thing better', and he cannot fail as long as he contains his efforts within the limits of popular conscience. People find it reassuring to be made to care about what they thought they already cared about. It is the fertile land of shared perceptions. The Theatre of Conscience is essentially a mass declaration of loyalty to moral principles. But it is not, as I believe art has to be, promiscuous. It is an activity that never sins.

Let me suggest that the theatre is literally a box, physically and morally a box. What occurs in the box is infinite because the audience wishes it to be infinite – there is no burden of proof at any moment. It is a black box, when the lights are off, because, as we all know, darkness permits the criminal and the promiscuous act. I wrote a play called *The Bite of the Night*. Darkness permits the thought, darkness licenses, it bites, and sometimes you can be bitten by love and sometimes by fear. When Brecht commanded that the box be filled with light he was driven by the passion for enlightenment, and he knew instructions require light just as the imagination hates light and flees from it. Imagination also flees its neighbours. In light you are only half-conscious of the stage and half-conscious of your neighbour. In all collective culture your neighbour controls you by his gaze. In darkness he is eliminated and you are alone with the actor. This is why the didactic play occurs in the street – street theatre is about teaching, black box theatre is about imagination. In the black box you are trusted to be free, to be solely responsible. To enter it is to be engulfed by the possibility of freedom through the powers of the actor and the dramatist, the onus is placed on the audience not as a collectivity, but as individuals. No disciplines, no recall to conscience. Because the box is hidden from the world, it owes as little as it wishes to the world, the rules in the box are different from the rules outside it. What else can explain the residual excitement we still experience in dark theatres? Why are we still a little half-afraid? Is it because we are about to watch an actor? Yes, because actors are not entirely human, but more, it is the sense of attending on a sin, the possibility of witnessing a transgression, the freedom to part with the necessary disciplines of the street, the possibility of acquiring that criminal perspective – not more enlightenment, but less. And of course, it is not you who sins, the actors sin for you. The box is a dangerous place, but you are not yourself physically in danger – all theatre that affronts or offends the audience by direct engagement wrecks that sacred compact between actor and witness that is older than history. To insult the audience for the paltry gratification of the actors destroys theatre, erodes its authority as an art, just as all invitations to debate what has been witnessed diminish its beauty. The great play is immune to discussion, the play eliminates debate, it is not about arguments, it replaces arguments.

A drama teacher, a pacifist, visited me. He told me of his production of *Antigone*, in which instead of a set he hung a massive map of the world on which every war currently being fought was illuminated by flaming red light. Of course, there were lots of these, and the actors played in the glare of them. At the end, he flung on the house lights and dragged chairs on to the stage, obliging the audience to engage in a debate on the so-called issues the production had raised. He therefore succeeded in eliminating the entire experience of the drama, humiliated the text by using it as a means to an end, a starting point for the endless curse of debating things, wrecked the invention of his actors, turning them into mere didactic instruments, and liquidated any possibility in the audience that their structure of feeling and thought could be inflamed by what they had witnessed – he had reduced the non-cerebral event of a play into a pack of arguments.

I repeat that the play is not a debate, it is literally 'play', and like children's play it is 'world-inventing', requiring no legitimation from the exterior. It is about impossibilities, and takes its immense spiritual authority from the simple question 'what if . . .?' not from the banal 'did you know . . .?' The question 'what if . . .?' immunizes the theatre from its worst enemies, the material researchers, who can devastate a documentary by flourishing a single fact. In black box theatre nothing can be challenged on the ground that it did not occur, or has no precedent. The response to the plaintive cry 'this could never happen!' is 'precisely, we are playing a play!' And play is dangerous, of course, it goes where it is not expected to go, it is quite simply immoral. When Hochhuth wrote his notorious play on Winston Churchill, the work was obscured – or it was intended to be – by a massive correspondence about the Churchillian archives. Hochhuth had 'researched' his play, but never well enough. By his meticulous realist method, he robbed his chosen art form of its major resource, and the whole event shifted from inside the theatre to outside it, to the columns of newspapers. If writers use theatre only as a means to get access to newspaper columns – what they call initiating debate – they vandalize theatre, they tear gaping holes in its walls through which a miserable daylight streams, showing us that actors are, after all, only people with painted faces.

It is my contention that theatre's power in the contemporary world ought to be much greater than it is, but that it has wilfully chosen to emasculate itself by imitating the habits of its rivals. Its writers are smitten with the idea of themselves as educators, and have subordinated actors to their wishes. They have made a theatre of morals almost as rigid as the medieval stage and have contributed to a new style of social conformism. They have told what they know, and have not dared to tread where they do not know, which is the authentic territory of a black box theatre. I also am a moralist, but not a puritan. By moralist I mean one who is tough with morality, who exposes it to risk, even to oblivion, and it is not for nothing I chose the theatre as my field because in essence the theatre is not a moral place, as our ancestors knew well when they intermittently banned it. It is a long time since anyone wanted to ban the theatre in this country, and that is itself suggestive. It is responsible, it is loyal, it is a willing collaborator in the enforcing of moral regulations. Let me for the last time return to the writer who thinks the purpose of his life and art is 'to make people understand one another'. I must admit that for many years when people asked me why I wrote, I resorted to such dismal platitudes myself, though with a deep sense of bad faith. I had a sense that art was a luxury and needed to be defended against charges of indulgence or privilege. In fact, I wrote because I needed to. I wrote for myself. But that seemed unforgivable. Only more recently did I understand that in writing for myself I also served others, and that, in not serving myself, I could not serve others. The more self-limiting an artist is, the less useful to his fellow human beings; the more he dares, the more he explores, and the more immoral he is, the better he serves. Then he or she becomes the enemy of collective lying. Then he or she runs the risk of seeing the work denied. Great art lives outside the moral system, and its audience, consciously or unconsciously, demands it, particularly in theatre whose very darkness is the condition of a secret pact, the pact of wilful infringement, of the suspension of conscience, between actor and audience. And the actor, as I suggested earlier, is not entirely human, nor do we wish him to be. He is not – and here as in most ways I totally reject the principles of community theatre – merely someone who might be in the audience on another night, the grocer in a funny hat, or your uncle pretending to be your ancestor – but quite other than us, gifted in special ways, not least in body and speech, particularly in speech; he has the gift of seducing – after all, dance is permitted everywhere, dance is the conformist act and ironically, repressive – but speech, that is the lost secret, and poetic speech is nearly religious in its power: not the humdrum repetition of naturalistic drama, but the rhythmic, undulating, journey of the articulated form known as 'the speech'. On the stage the actor is licensed to do the undoable, and he or she 'takes us out of ourselves' – a strangely accurate phrase that, like most common expressions, hides as much as it reveals. To be 'taken out of yourself' – the very thing demanded of the actor – is to be like the dog let off its lead, the lead being conscience, the lead being responsibility and loyalty. Like the dog, the actor experiences an atavistic moment of relief, wildness and barbarism, and even fear – for he is domesticated, after all – so we glimpse, with fear and delight, the landscape of a pre-moral world and are allowed to run in it. And what is the form of this landscape, for there is only one? It is tragedy. Impossible in comedy, for comedy is the suspension, the denial of emotion. The artist who dares to be tragic, the actor who is unafraid of tragedy, lives at the expense of his conscience, lives outside conscience. He sins for the audience, living on the very fringes of morality. This is the reason the actor in historic periods was banned, even in death, from hallowed ground – he was the player of the forbidden action, the manifestation of forbidden life. In a conscience-free theatre, there is, of course, no 'telling'. It is the farthest reach from the Brechtian demonstration. There is no 'telling' because the writer had nothing to tell – his play was a journey to him as it is a journey to the actor, the outcome of which was unknown at its beginning. It was for the writer a journey without maps whose destination might be an intemperate zone, a place of fear and little comfort. This is the very act of honouring that I have described elsewhere – the honouring of an audience by refusing the simple satisfactions of reiteration, affirmations, congratulation – the sort of theatre in which the morality was fixed in advance, and the writing, and the narrative was a means to an end. I repeat that the theatre tells nothing, and in a society where telling never stops, where news, political comment, advertising, the social debate, are a deafening cacophony, an orchestra of claims and counter-claims, all subject to the moral consensus of humanism, the theatre's sole and riveting power lies in its barbarism. Against the walls of the theatre there washes continuously the sea of morality and debate. The walls protect the actor and the audience not only from the racket of the street but also from its morality. Inside the black box, the imagination is wild and tragic and its criminality unfettered. The unspeakable is spoken. Here alone is the audience trusted with the full burden of what it has witnessed and liberated from the ideology of redemption, it witnesses in silence, a silence of pain, the terrible ambitions of the human spirit. Cruelty. Magnificence. Wrong actions. Instinct. Horror. Love beyond legality. When an audience witnesses such things beyond the structures of redemption or education, ideology or affirmation, it has recourse only to silence, a pathos which is perhaps a kind of self-pity permitted to a hero who finds himself, at last, alone.

The deconsecration of meaning in the Theatre of Catastrophe

The Theatre of Catastrophe refuses to endorse clarity as a principle of production in art. The question 'What is he saying?' cannot be applied to this theatre and is already a form of decadence. In this theatre the idea of 'saying' is redundant, just as the idea of clarity is seen to harbour an authoritarianism. In its place, we aim for a multiplicity of effects and a different form of theatrical experience. In this theatre the judgement that 'this play appears to have no meaning' is not felt as criticism. A new relation is forged between the audience and the stage which abolishes the idea of entertainment and the oppressive intellectual practices that this concept entails. Why have we come to this conclusion?

Firstly, the expectations aroused by three decades of political theatre have produced an intellectual servility in audiences. This servility is expressed in the desperate ache for the message, which denigrates the experience of art. Where the message is not evident the audience becomes resentful and the actors a target of contempt. This relation of audience and stage is a corrupt one since it implies knowledge to be a commodity, given by the dramatist to a fee-paying class.

Secondly, the discipline of political theatre eliminates complexity and contradiction, and massages its audience towards a futile celebration of prior knowledge. I mean by this the hidden assumption of shared morality which lies behind, for example, the idea of exposure. The political play has been relentless in its pursuit of exposure, the unveiling of conspiracies, the comic denigration of social types, political parties, etc., all of this resting on the sterile belief in a common morality, liberal-humanist, left-leaning, socially progressive.

Thirdly, the emphasis on clarity and realism has effectively abolished poetry from the stage, thereby colluding in the disfigurement of speech in the public arena and enthroning the journalist as the proprietor of truth. The theatre of clarity distrusts the audience it claims to serve, by denying them the right to experience the meaningless.

I want to discuss the idea of the meaningless play with reference to a number of works of my own produced principally by The Wrestling School or the Almeida Theatre, *The Possibilities*, *The Last Supper*, *Seven Lears*, but also some produced by national companies like the Royal Shakespeare such as *The Castle* and *The Bite of the Night*. These are the more recent plays in what I have characterized as a Theatre of Catastrophe, but some of the qualities of this type of drama are to be found in much earlier work, work which I believed at the time possessed a didactic or critical purpose.

What these plays have in common is their indigestibility. For all that they possess in terms of classic dramatic values, such as narrative, structure, character or language, they are irreducible to a set of meanings. The parables in *The Last Supper* and the ten plays of *The Possibilities* are not construable. This is not to say they are incomprehensible. They are merely narratives whose linkage to agreed moral structures is ruptured. This moral compact which has dominated the aesthetic environment of theatre in the last thirty years is abolished in the Theatre of Catastrophe and opens the prospect of a new relationship between the audience and the stage.

What do I think this relationship is, and how do I think it should be different? It is my judgement that the weakness of the contemporary theatre is its fear of the audience. The raked seating of most auditoria evokes the lecture hall or, worse, the jury box. The gratification of this potentially hostile mass, ranked above the actors in a position of critical dominance, is the first function of the performance. Leaving aside the commercial theatre, the idea of 'the success', even among radical companies, induces a predisposition to make compromises with the fullest demands of creative imagination which in theatre, as in any art, requires absolute licence. The horror that 'they' may not 'understand' the scene, that 'they' may lose the thread of the narrative, or that 'we' shall be accused of elitism if 'meaning' becomes obscure – and how this word 'obscure' is used to beat writers over the head – cripples the theatre with its false democracy. It is my view that behind the notions of 'clarity' and 'meaning' lies a contempt both for the audience and for the powers of imagination.

The disintegration of the liberal-humanist consensus offers scope for altering this governing aesthetic of production. In an age of excess, of entertainment, information, documentation and analysis, the theatre gains nothing by competing with superior technologies. A theatre of social analysis, dependent on the communication of ideas and, consequently, on a permanent narrative of meaning, treats its audience like a dog on a lead. The terror felt by an audience deprived of such a narrative is akin to the shock felt by an animal uncaged – it is hesitant, even resistant, to the prospect of its own freedom. In the Theatre of Catastrophe the deal under which the audience resigns its rights to the domination of the author in exchange for information or entertainment, conscience or massage, is abolished. The first signal that no such compact exists comes from the unfamiliar cadences of a new language, whose rhythms and syntax are not those of common speech. It is a speech as contrived as poetry, dislocated, sometimes lyrical, often coarse, whose density and internal contradictions both evoke and confuse. In a culture in which language has lost its public status in favour of image and selling, this flood of verbal sound overwhelms the listener, who must be content with a partial understanding but whose attention is fixed by the sensuality of substance of speech in the mouth of the trained actor. It has been often remarked that my theatre is predominantly an actors' theatre, and it is certainly true that actors have been my greatest allies and collaborators. This reflects the supreme responsibility that is placed in them, in their powers of articulation to conduct what is in effect a symphony of speech. It is this displacement of attention from meaning to texture that characterizes the first moments of the play. The actors' seduction of the audience, which, as in any seduction, is achieved by means other than the rational, is crucial to the renewal of, and the renegotiation of, the terms of the theatre.

I have said that the existing theatre, with its configuration of stage and seating, inhibits the unblocking of imagination by its mute assertion of power. By collectively situating the audience in blocks who peer into the pit of the stage, or even gaze down a raked landscape of seats, this is a theatre which implies a unanimity of response. I have said elsewhere that one of the most depressing sounds in the theatre is that of the audience in the unified pursuit of a single goal – the laugh, for example – which is so easily achieved. I regard this as an essentially servile relationship on both sides of the lights – the performers and authors who are gratified to have struck a seam of unanimity – and the audience who sense they have achieved value for money. A more complex and creative theatre uses moments of unanimity only to achieve more startling effects of division, in which the audience is atomized and in which the laugh, where it occurs, is accompanied by a sense of the faux pas, or where it comes unbidden, from amazement that comedy exists at all. The possibility of the audience feeling itself at liberty to respond individually to what it witnesses – its liberation from the shackles of meaning – can be properly cultivated only in a theatre which is not one.

Our task is to make theatre a necessity. This can be achieved only when what it provides ceases to be entertainment on the one hand, or moral or political instruction on the other. In the Theatre of Catastrophe its powers of reconciliation or resolution are abolished in favour of a passionate assertion of human complexity which cannot be distorted by ideology or shaped by the goodwill of humanist collectivity. The new audience that has appeared for this theatre is not oppressed by the absence of meaning or the threat of obscurity. Both these terms, along with the accusation of pessimism, are regarded by such an audience as critical barriers erected to sustain the existing economy of stage/audience relations. We live in an age of persistent meaning, of relentless indoctrination, not only from the state, but from the artistic community, the commercial empires and the propagandist forces of an information network. The status of news – which includes opinion – has never been greater. The theatre must resolutely defy the persuasive logic of news and return the rights of interpretation to the audience. In this freedom from the oppression of meaning audiences will discover the necessity of theatre as a multitude of possibilities in which the constant imperative of judgement is willingly surrendered.

When I talked to an audience of students after the first performance of *The Last Supper* in 1988, I was subjected to a tirade of abuse from a young man who had found the evening deeply discomforting. This abuse was directed at me, and not at the actors, whose performances, he was compelled to admit, were beyond reproach. The substance of his complaint was that he felt foolish, and was humiliated, by the absence of meaning in the play. His intellect, trained in methods of analysis, and his experience, formed from the endless narratives of televisual realism, rebelled against the play's deflective surfaces. He had paid money to be taught, and the actors had taught him nothing, other than the power of acting. At least, so it appeared to him. I argued that this anger, which in its violence revealed profound disturbance, was a symptom of a struggle he was obliged to undertake to emerge from a servile relationship he experienced with theatre, from which he demanded product in the form of knowing where I stood. Once he knew where I stood, he would be satisfied. I could not say where I stood. As long as I had known where I stood, I produced inferior theatre, intent on demonstrating my thesis. Instead I offered in this play the experience, which was itself the purpose of the evening's work. And I use the word *work* deliberately, since the work is not only the actors', but also the audience's. The play is a landscape in which the audience is encouraged to wander without maps. It is marked, it is not chaotic, but the disciplines of this theatre do not include the disciplines of demonstration. I am glad to say this student's bitterness was not common to the others. Many said they abandoned, or struggled to abandon, their demands, early in the play, some as soon as the invitation arrived in the form of the prologue. Once this discarding had occurred, they were able to immerse themselves in the actions, moving from scene to scene fluidly, refusing to be stuck on points of loss or obvious contradiction. In this they found an appetite for theatre which was not diminished by the fact that they made no claim to 'understand' it. Because we played in a conventional theatre, this movement was harder to achieve. Physically they had encountered the play in seats, pampered as consumers. They had not expected to work, let alone to suffer. Everything conspired to make them pass judgement on what failed to entertain them. They overcame these conditions in an alliance with a company of actors whose faith was infectious.

For the theatre to regain the initiative in a society which offers a superfluity of dramatic product it must address itself to its own uniqueness. This entails the creation of structures in both language and narrative that do not owe their legitimacy to representation of the world beyond the stage. The audience must feel what it witnesses is beyond what it conceives to be common experience. In my play *The Bite of the Night* a classics teacher at a defunct university, having driven his father to suicide and his son into vagrancy, takes his favoured pupil Hogbin on a reluctant tour of the Eleven Troys of antiquity, engaging with Helen in a succession of political systems each of which reduces her physically until she is no more than a voice in a chair. The ahistoricity of this journey is obvious, the collapsing of time and narrative signalling to the audience that it must forsake its conventional expectations of meaning, and the interventions of scenes of interlude which bear only obliquely on the main action, encouraging it to suspend its urge to organize the material until the conclusion of the performance. Beyond this, each act of this three-act play opens with a prologue whose poetic discursiveness lends only the most slender connections in terms of meaning to the act about to follow, but which draw the audience further away from its organizational instincts into a form of surrender to an intensity of dramatic experience which stimulates its imaginative involvement to a point at which it is overwhelmed. This play has a performance time of about five hours. The Royal Shakespeare Company felt it necessary to issue an apology for the length of this experience, thereby confessing its inability to trust theatre when it failed to commoditize itself properly. In its struggle to contain the power of drama in its contest with the greater conveniences of television or film, the State theatre condemns theatre to irrelevance, eroding the very bases of its uniqueness.

The cult of accessibility and the Theatre of Obscurity

There are two critical terms which have become, in regard to my own work, the definitive signals of approval or hostility. One of these is a neologism, the other is as old as criticism itself. One is a catchword of a corrupt political culture and the other a respectable concept which has been annexed in a desperate search for a derogatory terminology. I refer to those two poles of contemporary judgement, accessibility and obscurity.

The first of these is by no means limited to theatre, or even to art itself. We hear about the need for 'access' to museums, 'access' to spaces, 'access' to the countryside, to education, to information, even to knowledge itself. There is nothing, apparently, to which 'access' cannot be applied. This liberal-sounding criterion conceals a profound suspicion of the imagination behind a fashionable hatred of privilege. All things that are not accessible must be privileged, the theory runs, all spaces that are hidden are ipso facto the preserves of an elite, and all ideas or works of art that fail to communicate themselves are – obscure. In this sham democracy, it is not only the entire stock of the culture that must be thrown open, or vilified, there is an obligation laid on the living artist to make himself 'understood'. Thus with regard to my own work, the play which receives the approval of the critical regime is first and foremost the 'accessible' one, whose narrative is simple, whose characters are rapidly absorbed, identified and classified as 'good' or 'bad', and whose momentum can be contained within the 'issue', in this case the 'issue' of artistic freedom and State patronage. This constricting and oppressive critical straitjacket, with its hatred for abstraction, threatens writers, musicians, museum administrators and doubtless, in future, philosophers, too.

Those who are threatened by the dictat of accessibility, 'Be understood or Perish', need to keep their nerve, since in a populist culture the abuse from certain quarters is bound to become increasingly violent. The writer of 'inaccessible' theatre will be repudiated

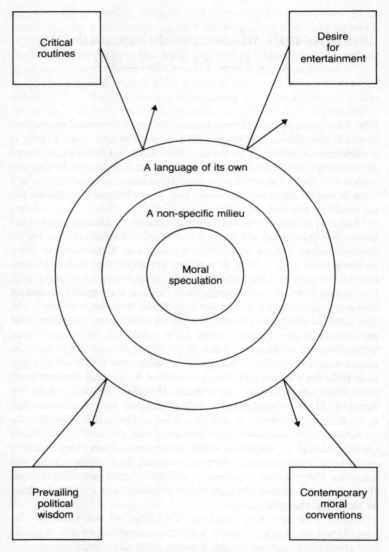

Plan for the fortification of an imaginative work

as a poseur, or, most favoured of all English calumnies, identified as 'pretentious'. His collaborators will be seen as dupes, the actors vilified as brainless exhibitionists, and the institution which mounts the production attacked as corrupt, elitist and overdue for demolition.

Theatrical experience as pure commodity entails frontal attacks of this kind on all work which does not yield instant meaning, meaning which is frequently no more than narrative itself – hence the emphasis on 'structure' in reactionary practice, 'real life' and such-like. The theatre's historic bondage to the idea of 'entertainment' has ensured that alternative experiences of theatre lack even a proper vocabulary for their expression. We have all experienced the conversation which begins 'Did you enoy that play . . . ?' and the response, 'Well, I don't think *enjoy* is exactly the word . . .', but what is the word? The accessible play poses no such problems for the critic or the audience. Its problem and its solution are one and the same. It reiterates the conventional opinion much as my own play *Scenes from an Execution* reiterates the belief that artists tell the truth, a very dubious and, of course, circular opinion. What this play, and all 'accessible' plays, do is to exist within moral certitudes. I think it is safe to say that no accessible play denies the moral burden of the climate in which it is created. In its exigesis it affirms the reigning moral consensus, no matter what the shocks it delivers en route. In this fatal bond between imagination and existent morality, the play about 'issues' becomes the most 'relevant', 'important' and 'accessible' of all theatre, since it can operate only in a field of shared morality. Michael Billington, a critic more obsessed with the accessible than most, forlornly pleads that I should address myself to 'contemporary issues', as if here, at least, consensus must be restored. Here is articulated – out of despair at 'obscurity' – the suffocating insistence of liberal-humanist ideological solidarity.

Accessibility demands that whatever our differences we must speak a common tongue (usually street naturalism) and share a common morality. It also invites, without necessarily stating the necessity for, the old reactionary quality of celebration. But what about a theatre that repudiates this? Or indeed any art that declines to share in the governing notions of 'goodness', 'importance' or 'relevance'? What are its characteristics? The first will be – yes – its 'obscurity'. For such a theatre will hardly announce itself in terms of clarity, since nothing is clear here, least of all morality. And, yes, the author will certainly not be in 'command of his material', most of which will be – yes – 'undigested'. His thoughts will certainly be disorganized, and he will certainly appear 'not to know what he is doing'. He will not know how to structure a play, let alone make it well-made, and, what is more, will, in a spasm of shocking elitism, appear to be 'wrestling with his own demons', the very antithesis of the accessible play, where authors grapple with everybody else's demons. This is the theatre of selfishness, and its maker is someone who sees himself or herself unashamedly as an artist, the power of whose imagination is their sole claim on public attention. This is a theatre whose business is not 'communication' at all, but expression. To the pains and triumphs of this instinct which makes no compromise with moral responsibility, an audience comes which demands the very thing in shortest supply in a populist regime of culture – complexity, contradiction, pain and absence – the precious silence born of the absence of both solutions and moral exhortation. In this theatre all is obscurity, since nothing is known, it is relentlessly speculative, and its judgements are made, if at all, in the days and weeks following performance, never in the experience itself.

In this theatre also, the ingrained habits of seeing and hearing as a means to the construction of meaning are suspended – and surprisingly easily for many people. Images are relished for themselves, and language becomes a sensuality, like the voice of the actor itself. The entire onus of meaning, the super-objective of the Stanislavsky school, is displaced from the stage on to the audience which feels either betrayed or exhilarated; cheated or honoured; tricked out of its conventional rewards or looted in the private recesses of its soul. 'What did it mean . . . ?' – that melancholy cry of an audience sent away without its message or the satisfaction of seeing 'real life' – is discovered to be an archaic question, a rudimentary response to a cultural oppression, or a populist spasm of amour-propre on the part of an audience whose members until then have liked to think of artists as 'just like them', articulators of their problems and witnesses of their lives.

I have called this a Theatre of Catastrophe, but it might as well be a Theatre of Obscurity in its abolition of the moral compact which underlies the 'accessible' play. It is a theatre of powerful disciplines, nevertheless, and by no means a torrent of unconsciousness. Very obvious transgressions occur which make it deeply unsympathetic to existing practice – the first of these being its irresponsibility. It is one of the planks of a liberal-humanist theatre that its artists are

[88]

responsible, men and women of conscience and social purpose. I am bound to say the exclusion of my work from the National Theatre of England in the past 18 years can only reflect its hidden moral function – common to all national theatres by definition – 'the serving of the community', as if the community were served by conscience in the first place. It is certainly one of the flawed conventions of my accessible play *Scenes from an Execution* that the protagonist, the artist Galactia, with whom all critics find it easy to sympathize, is a pacifist. I am inclined to wonder how the play might have been received if I had had the courage and imagination to present her as an apologist for violence. I have another play, *The Bite of the Night*, in which the protagonist incites his father to suicide and collaborates in the dismemberment of a woman, Helen of Troy. This play is described by Michael Billington as 'enragingly obscure'. Let the first rule of the Obscure Theatre therefore be its repudiation of virtue, that debilitating sense that the author is 'on our side', 'one of us', and ready and willing to 'nail the enemy', with his persistent wit.

The pleasures of the Obscure Theatre are, I suggest, to be found in precisely those areas which give rise to such anxiety amongst the lovers of accessibility, and the conflict I have attempted to outline is a long and fundamental quarrel over the nature and function of art itself. The common aspiration of every writer in every medium is that his work should 'create new perceptions'. This weary formula sounds less convincing with every telling. What does it mean, and how does this peculiar phenomenon occur? If it does occur, how can it be compatible with 'access'? I cannot for a moment pretend I have ever written for a public whom I judged in need of enlightenment. I have never wanted to 'tell' anything to anyone, or wished to alter their views on any subject. I was always engaged with the problems of my own psyche and the tensions within my own personality. The theatre I have chosen to embrace is one which makes no compact with its audience as to entertainment, ideological instruction, humanist celebration or changed perceptions. As the artist chiefly responsible for what occurs on the stage I claim no superior insight or even the status of a visionary, let alone a just man with a conscience. My obscurity is precisely the result of sacrificing these claims to attention, and an act of pure irresponsibility, and I justify my theatre not by its contribution to a humanist culture – a celebration of the essential goodness of the man animal – but precisely by its suspension of morality. There are no good people in these plays, nor is happiness posited as an end at all; reconciliation fails to arrive, or is disrupted, and love is a manifestation of cruelty. In this apparent pessimism, which is pessimism only to those schooled in the official doctrine of optimism, the appeal can never be to conscience, but only to the undeniable power of pain in the imagination, the play being open not to a single interpretation, but to many, with the resulting appetite for re-viewing which characterizes the audience of this work. No one sees *Scenes from an Execution* twice, but they come back to *Seven Lears*, as they returned to *The Bite of the Night*, not in search of the meaning I have hidden in the undergrowth of the text, but to make it for themselves. For them, 'accessibility' is now the tedium of a servile art.

A bargain with impossibility: the theatre of moral speculation in an age of accord*

One of the uglier clichés of artistic production in a culture such as ours is the routine justification of effort by results. The complicity between artist and critic achieves an unhealthy apotheosis in the reiteration of the phrase – invented to sustain a dominant cultural myth – that such and such a work of art 'changed perceptions', as if in some delightfully painless way society edged towards ever greater civility by virtue of watching plays or observing pictures. You can hear this uttered as both the ultimate critical accolade, and the self-conscious artist's anxious plea for justification in an age of relentless utilitarianism. If his duty is to entertain, his reward is the knowledge that his dramatic skills inflicted upon his audience some collective shift of focus. But what does it mean, this labouring to 'change perceptions'? It serves to incorporate artists and actors into a social consensus of conscience and critique, and bestows on them a spurious respectability – it is redolent of earnestness, responsibility, legislative/poetic romanticism, the sort of fake heroism that now attaches to journalists of the investigative kind and has infected drama with its relentless exposés of yet further scandals that merely confirm – what? – our mutual fascination with corruption? our common desire to humiliate the rich? Dramatists may pursue the fallacy of 'changed perceptions' to a point of exhaustion – except that there is no point of exhaustion in an art which is both inspired and justified by the desire to affirm a popular morality. Man is the social animal whose antics reward permanent observation, but the price of an art of conscience is a stage peopled by characters who cannot achieve autonomy, and therefore do not operate at the imaginative level – they are observed, not invented. There is great safety and security to be enjoyed in the exchange of conscience-ridden observations, affirmations of shared values, humanistic platitudes, but the

* George Orwell Memorial Lecture, Birkbeck College, 4 December 1991.

[91]

D

stage remains essentially sterile, and the insistence on the representation of what passes for the real world only enhances the decadent sense of social responsibility whilst devastating the landscape of dramatic invention.

The entire spectrum of theatre is susceptible to this culture of justification by results, the utilization for collectively respectable ends of an art form once suspiciously irrational in its origins and effects, and this annexation has its origins in Shaw, Brecht and the Enlightenment dramatists like Lessing. We now enjoy a unanimity of functional intention that extends from the wildest performance arts to the most highly-invested language theatre of the National – the cultural accord is total. The well-intentioned children of the Welfare State have grown into cultural producers of social critiques for both mass and minority audiences. Behind their spectacular or routine dramatic methods lies the spectacle of relentless harmony – it has become impossible any longer actually to *resent* the artistic experience, to feel any resistance to it per se, since like Chekhov's character Astrov in *Uncle Vanya* it is so profoundly permeated with idealism that dissonance is prostrated. Who could disagree that we are living an ecological disaster? Who would choose to defend the legal profession or the art market? We swim a tepid bath of humanistic accord, writer, actor, audience, an alliance of foregone conclusions which diminishes the possibility of innovative practice.

What I am describing is in effect a collusion between the populist State – defined by the near-identity of the political programme no matter which party articulates it – and a theatre no longer able to live its radical functions as they were expressed, say, in the 1960s and 1970s – a theatre which prided itself on its contribution to a debate, and fatally diminished itself in the process. What we now witness is such an accord between art and society that it is impossible to distinguish (in moral terms) the work of grossly over-funded national theatres – which are simply artistic arms of the national conscience – and the theatre of the margins. The drama of conscience reigns virtually unopposed, and the aspiration to 'change perceptions' is welcome on all sides of the political spectrum – if it is a spectrum at all. It is a further aspect of modern populism that everyone is entitled to complain at injustice, even to pursue it in the full glare of publicity, and the clean sweep of the humanist regime incorporates entertainers and critics alike. In a drama emerging from a process of empirical research, the source of inspiration is inevitably indignation at malpractice, and there is neither a threat to order nor, more significantly, any possible extension of experience in a realist project of this kind. What occurs is the routine massaging of collective values that passes for 'communication', communication being territorial familiarity, acts of recognition, the stimulation of sympathy with the catalogue of known and revered victims. It is a theatre whose heroic period consisted in the annexation of common experience, but whose decadence consists in its fixed embrace of common morality.

I would like to propose a different theatre, in which conscience is removed from its dominant function and criticism is confined to that fatal axis where it alone operates to the common good – that which lies between the artist and the text, the self-criticism exercised in deletion, excision, self-denial of the banal and the routine. I would like to propose that the value of works of art, in social circumstances such as the present, lies not in their entertainment value, nor in their ability to 'change perceptions' in pursuit of some common purpose, but in their power to devastate the received wisdom of the collective, which conspires to diminish individual experience at all levels. A theatre which addresses the individual and ceases to regard the audience as an entity, which denies the existence of the audience as singular at all, must above all things be irresponsible and disloyal. It cannot hope for the status of social critic, since the social critic is fully incorporated, and it must not clamour for the comforts of solidarity, the much-vaunted 'celebration' of the community play or the musical, for these are the realm of the commercial or the politically facile. It is in the rupturing of these ties – essentially the breaking of the curse of entertainment – that the prospect of a new theatre lies. Formal innovations in theatre – the slide towards anti-literary theatre, anti-linguistic theatre – will not solve what is, in essence, an impasse created by excessive harmony. The action of such a form of drama will not be to labour to 'widen sympathy' or 'to make us understand one another better', another element of the catechism of the humanist theatre, but rather the opposite, to engender division, to weaken spurious ties, to provoke a sense of incurable alienation from the polis which alone can give us access to the authentic experience of tragedy – for the pursuit of harmony and unity (the sentimental ambition of artists and, to some extent, their sole licence) abolished tragedy in the fond pursuit of rational order and spiritual peace. The relations of such a radical theatre with the 'real world' – observed reality and common territory – are not those

[93]

of the documentary observer who hauls on to the stage – and in daylight, by theory – the 'problem' or the 'issue' of a given subject, but are fugitive from it and in pursuit of the hidden, the unarticulated material of the psyche where it *confronts* reality. It is primarily a speculative art – a bargain with impossibility – since it is not subject to empirical truth and denies the critique of realism at every turn. The power of conviction in writer and performer are its own justifications, enabling individuals in the audience to cross the threshold of reality principles and trespass where morality is insecure. The bargain between the stage and the audience is struck not a priori by common principles but between individuals in pursuit of imaginative reconnoitre. This crucial point of rupture with governing principles of politics and morality is its distinguishing characteristic, and it entails – something I am not able to enter into here – new manners of performance since the governing models of the contemporary theatre – still wholly Stanislavskian and Brechtian in nature – are rigorously anti-speculative, obsessed with intentions and objectives, and oppressive in their severe delimitations of stage action and actors' invention.

The title of this paper, 'A bargain with impossibility', derives from a poem written by me in response to an incident that occurred here at Birkbeck some years ago following the showing of my television play *Pity in History*. It refers to the compact which exists between an imaginative art and its audience. The reaction of an old soldier, who appeared to have wandered in from the street, bedecked with medals which clearly demonstrated his rights to his own history – his empirical authority, so to speak, to debate the subject of war and injury – was profoundly hostile to the portrayal of a dying army cook played – with characteristic energy – by the actor Ian McDiarmid. This old soldier's bitterness underlined for me the poverty of the common perception of theatre and its responsibilities that now dominates the realist discourse. The poem, which is titled 'Men don't die like that', takes this rebuke as its starting point.

Men don't die like that

> The tramp would thrash me with his memory
> For showing death like this*
> Would lay his scourge of anger down my back

Ten for impertinence
Ten for irreverence
Ten for failing to observe the facts

His medals jangle like drunk girls
His grave mouth gapes for oaths to
Satisfy a violated piety

Suffering lends him authority which he
Transports like an archbishop's hat

He knows
He saw
He yells

Men don't die like that

No use pleading my method
To list theatre's bargains with impossibility
Would be a waste of breath
This high priest of experience can't be gainsaid
He swings his pain over my head

   The
     Unrepentant
       Stager
        Of
         Discord

For I

Though my speculation cruelly offends
Concede nothing to the recollectionist
Knowing fidelity would pulp the heart of art
More savagely than shells did his friends

Decades of naturalistic drama – and the political and social values
that attach to it – had taught this individual member of the audience
that the sole purpose of showing an action on stage was to achieve
the highest proximity to human experience, and that any deviation
from it constituted an offence against the collective – was in effect,
lying. What I was groping towards in plays of that period within the
body of my own work was an emphatic disassociation, a rupture,
between stage and reality, in effect a licence to lie, which had,

* *Pity in History*, BBC TV, 1985.

indeed, long existed in the history of the theatre but which had been revoked. I wanted to take advantage of fiction, to permit more articulation than nature would permit, simply, to *exaggerate*, and to do so with a form of language that was – despite the actor's ease – contrived, dense, poetic, in a way common speech rarely can be, so both the content and the mode of expression were unhindered by considerations of truth-to-life. This, of course, is no more than a description of dramatic method before the nineteenth century, but there are times when the reoccupation of abandoned aesthetic territory is the point of departure for more significant developments.

If the Theatre of Conscience and Criticism – as I think one might characterize the best post-war British theatre – renounced poetic language as artificial, it also attempted to demolish the walls of the theatre, a laudable enough aim when those walls filtered pain from patrons bent on escapism and the perpetuation of images of leisured life – when they were, in effect, protecting the audience from experience by reproducing the ethic of drawing-room society. But nothing is immune from its own processes of decay, and it is my contention that a theatre without walls, a theatre which – metaphorically – exists in the street, having once liberated imagination, now stifles it, and that the fact of its privileged space is now its greatest lever on curiosity, and both its walls and darkness permit a freedom from the moral consensus not tolerated elsewhere. To persist with the metaphor, the walls symbolically and actually define freedom within, and the darkness permits precisely the atomization of the audience that Brecht so longed to forbid, preferring *his* audience to sit in white light and thereby discipline and educate each other, under the enlightened control of the author. The bargain I want to define is therefore one in which the audience individual demands of the dramatist not the reiteration of collective values, the narrative which is suspended from the threads of popularly held beliefs, but the relentless speculation on morality which touches only at points on the familiar, which invokes the real world only in order to dislocate it. This is the country of Obscurity where the common equipment of critical judgement – at least as understood in the contemporary theatre – finds no place. The criteria of the humanist critic, related almost entirely to utilitarian standards – mutual understanding, social benefit, enhancement of life within certain narrow boundaries – can no more apply to a theatre of this kind than can an actor trained in naturalistic techniques and nurtured on televisual realism perform its language. It is, in its first principles, a theatre which invents a world rather than representing one, and it is, furthermore, relentlessly tragic. In other words, it is a theatre of pain, but one without obligations to reconciliation or harmony.

Tragedy is possible only in cultures secure enough to tolerate the performance of infringements against collective wisdom. Insecure cultures shelter in the penumbra of moral certainty, reiterated with diminishing conviction on stages of extreme moral propriety – is it possible to conceive of a theatre more fixed and sclerotic with propriety than the National Theatre of England? This propriety is, of course, characterized by an adherence to the socio-critical play, whether it is a routine revival of Fo's *Accidental Death* or star vehicle texts like Brecht's *Arturo Ui* whose satirical targets are safely confined to the nostalgic era, and it is perhaps hardly worth making the observation that national theatres reproduce national ideologies, whatever idealist propaganda may have attended on their births. My point is a simple one, that the breadth of the moral compact, which is itself a sign of profound social unease, makes the writing of tragedy an act of *lèse majesté*; the imagining of the forbidden, with the aesthetic principles that might accompany it – invented language, speeches whose content is destabilizing of the actor's conventional method, being digressionary, contradictory within the span of a sentence, and with no objectives at all – is the negation of naturalism, the negation of satire, of cheer-leading, enemy-identifying and, above all, the negation of the post-Chekhovian, suburban self-hatred that permeates late humanist theatre at this time in this country.

A theatre of tragedy makes its end the very opposite of the end of entertainment – it complicates life, and sends its audience away with that faint grudge at having been troubled at a level beneath the consciously moral. It displaces the simple gratifications of 'A good night out', and insists on the exposure of pain that is not soluble. It makes no attempt to 'change perceptions' at all, not regarding that as its business, but arrives at the compact with its audience from a different perspective, that of the deal struck between writer and audience that here at least nothing will be banned, in the interests of either taste or unity, nor will the illicit thought be so treated in dramatic terms as to enable us to dispose of it. There will be no enlightenment dispensed. It is *transgression* that lies at the heart of tragic experience, not accident; it is Lear's howling rebukes to a world without morality that excite us, not his civilizing; it is the heroic actions of his misjudgement that excite our curiosity and not his apology – a dénouement that is the exercise of Christian charity, and an act of will, just as the bloody conclusions of so many Jacobean tragedies are no more than the genuflection of imagination to legality, a debt paid by an artist to a semi-tolerant State.

It is this relation between the dreamer and the State that forms the subject of my own play *The Europeans*, commissioned by the Royal Shakespeare Company in 1985 and due to receive its first professional performance in a production by The Wrestling School in 1993. Set in the liberated Austria of 1683, and taking as its background the struggle in Central Europe against Islamic imperialism, the protagonist is the victim of an atrocity who refuses to forgive, and in her intrepid will to live her pain in public profoundly offends the reconciliatory State. She is a screaming exhibit in the Museum of Reconciliation. The following speech is delivered on a wasteland near Vienna where a youthful bishop has been discovered in the act of burying the body of his mother, whom he has just murdered. The Empress of Austria, a woman of profound curiosity, insists he justifies the act of matricide by preaching a sermon to the assembled labourers and troops.

The MEN *reluctantly form a circle.* ORPHULS *prepares, and then with the force of inspiration, turns to deliver his oration.*

ORPHULS. All that occurs, does it not occur that I should be its beneficiary, nourished on it, be it filth or excellence? Even the death of love is food to the soul and therefore what is evil? Is there evil except not to do? I do not blaspheme when I say the gift of life is paltry and our best service to God is not to thank Him, endless thanking, no, but to enhance His offer, and yet you do not, I think if I were God I would declare with some weariness or even vehemence, how little they do with the breath I gave them, they exhale repetitions, they applaud the lie, they sleep even in their waking hours, why did I make them thus, I erred in some respect, they fill me with disgust, have you no notion of God's horror? I am thinking of the God in us whose profound groan is the background to our clatter – (*He identifies one of the uncomprehending* WORKMEN.) You shake your head in silence, is that freedom? If silence was freedom it is so no longer, the word is volatile, am I too difficult for you? **Liar! You hide behind the so-called simplicity of Christ, but is that not a blasphemy?** (*Pause.*) If I had not done evil, how could I address you who have perhaps thought evil only? If I did not know cruelty could I know pity, they are the twin towers of the soul? Do not hold hands in

[98]

false gestures as if by crowding you could exclude the groan of God, no, you must hear the sound of His despair, and we must learn from Judas whose Gospel is not written, we must learn from him who stood alone, for Judas did not sell Christ nor was he corrupt, but Judas was cruel for knowledge, and without Judas there could be no resurrection, Beauty, Cruelty, and Knowledge, these are the triple order of the Groaning God, I speak as your adviser in whose pain you may see beauty, I praise my beauty and you must praise yours! (*Pause.*) I end here, in a proper and terrible exhaustion, I have laid myself before you, which is the duty of a priest. (*Pause.*)

EMPRESS. How wonderful you are . . . I shall not forget one word you said. How wonderful you are, I could truly love you. But we can't know that, and you must die . . . mustn't he? (*She looks at* LEOPOLD. *The bell of a great church.*)

It is precisely in the hinge between the independence of moral will, claimed and performed, and the crushing imperatives of public order and its necessary pieties, that a drama of moral speculation discovers its resources, and fractures the repression of experience that characterizes a culture industry such as we enjoy, bent on extinguishing pain in a welter of comedy and the inflation of domestic routine into seamless narratives. If it is true, as Adorno suggested, that no great art is ever socially desired, its corollary must be that the desired is an art that contributes only to the restatement of the given. In a series of ten plays called *The Possibilities* that were performed for the first time at the Almeida Theatre in 1986, I attempted to write a set of short narratives that could not be claimed by the audience on the usual territory of moral accord. These included the story of a peasant who would not abandon serfdom even when freedom was forced upon him by his master, a bookseller who believed books were too precious to be wasted on the public, and, in the particular one that follows, a torturer who is possessed of rather more sensibilities than his victims. He arrives in search of lodgings at the house of a woman who has herself been the victim of torture and, as a consequence, has lost the power of speech.

A widow's house. A MAN *arrives with a bag of tools.* THE WOMAN *is seated.*

THE TORTURER. They said if I came here you would have a room. Have you a room? (*She looks at him.*) You have a room? You have a room but you don't know if you like me? Understandable. I am not local and the accent's odd. Perhaps I'm dirty from the road? I'll pay in advance. Or rather, as I have no money yet, I will give you the toolbag as a pledge.

(*He puts the bag down.*) They say they pay on Fridays. What do you say? I am a foreigner, but though I am in many ways unlike you, in others I am identical, so we might progress from there. (*She just looks.*) I don't know what your silence means. I have come across many silent people, but in the end, they spoke. Perhaps that is how it will be with you. I am a skilled man and eat a light breakfast. Also, I sleep soundly and bring no friends back to my lodgings. I am not solitary, but neither am I convivial. What do you say? I won't plead for a room. I would rather lie in a ditch than plead. I am proud, which is perhaps my single fault. (*Pause. He picks up the bag.*) All right, I haven't satisfied you. (*He starts to go, then stops.*) Ah, now I remember. You are deaf and dumb! They told me at the castle, she lets rooms but she is deaf and dumb. Now I have made us both feel foolish! (*He laughs. Pause.*) I am the torturer from Poland and I have been offered a post at the castle. The new lord said there could be no more torture it was against his conscience and dismissed the old one, who, like me, set off across the country in search of a new post. But after six months, the necessity for torture made itself apparent, as it always does, and execution also could not be done without for long, so it was my luck to knock at his gate when the vacancy existed and the need was obvious to all. I have references from previous employers, all of whom were sorry to see me go, but I am a wanderer. I love to travel and I know my trade is never low for long, now shall I go up you unpleasant hag I detest the sight of you and one interview in a day is quite enough. Your eye is fixed on mine like a crow on dying vermin and I know your rooms all stink.

The woman's son, whilst pretending to admire the lodger, plans to murder him in revenge for the agony she has endured, but the torturer is quicker, kills the son, and replaces him in the affections of the mother. The unpredictability of these relationships, and the removal of the elements of moral sympathy that normally dictate the shape of a narrative, made these plays both difficult and fascinating for the audience. A profound resentment at the failure of the evening to deliver affirmations of the familiar kind was coupled with a peculiar will to see it through, a sense of endurance not blandished by platitudes of the 'changed perceptions' variety. It was difficult, and insoluble. It was not a puzzle, however, the satisfactions of it were not cerebral. It was emotional, and it displaced meaning from the confines of the narrow language of 'author's objectives' back to the audience itself. Individuals in the audience could not complain of being cheated, since the terms of the artistic bargain were fulfilled in every respect – the plays were complete in themselves, the characters achieved full autonomy, but somewhere, a convention had been levered out of place, leaving a sense of absence, such as one crossing an arch would balk at the missing keystone. This keystone was moral accord.

A similar impossibility in the architecture of a play characterizes the ruthless pursuit of Helen of Troy in my very much longer play, *The Bite of the Night*, given by the Royal Shakespeare Company at the Pit in 1988. At five hours long, this was deemed such an affront to human tolerance that the RSC box office were given instructions to dissuade potential customers by prefacing all ticket sales with details of its length and obscenity. Some nevertheless found the courage to defy this health warning and expose themselves to what was, if nothing else, a *tour de force* of sustained acting invention by Nigel Terry, about whose extraordinary performance I have written at length elsewhere (pp. 63–64). The narrative is disrupted by the inclusion of act-prologues (pp. 40–44) and scenes of digression, stage poems whose relation to the main action is – a Stanislavskian nightmare – at best peripheral. On top of this, the play moves between times. Thus, the protagonist's academic fascination with Helen of Troy – he is the last classics teacher at a defunct university somewhere in England – is made practical by a series of appalling acts of impiety which, taken together, serve to liberate him and his student into the classical world at the point where Troy has fallen and Helen, restored to her husband, begins her terrible descent. Helen is made the collective's scapegoat for the failure of the eleven societies that are erected on Troy's ruins, but it is Dr Savage, Ph.D., who is the evil genius for all her suffering, the inventor of all her punishments, and the eventual undertaker of her few remains. However, as I explained above, his licence originates in the scattering and destruction of his own family – that contemporary totem – which he achieves in a single afternoon, by a series of inspirations. His child he hands over to a sinister visitor, and his father – the Anchises of the piece – he persuades to commit suicide by suggesting he has been a burden on his own creativity. In other words, it is playing love *against* the family bond that persuades the old man to do away with himself. The vistas of repression that lie behind the debts of family love make this scene simultaneously fascinating and repulsive and set the play off in a condition of *moral suspension* that gives the audience a necessary indication of what is to come. In this scene Dr Savage, watching his weeping child part from him for the last time in the hand of a stranger, sees his chance to disburden himself of the old man too. The old man, loyal to the end, is carrying Savage's dinner on a plate. He watches the child depart, a small bag with flannel and toothbrush in his hand. He assumes he is off to a sporting event.

OLD MAN. Football, is it? (*He puts the plate down, starts to go.*)

SAVAGE. I owe you nothing, do I? (*He stops.*) Because you grated on my mother, what's the debt?

OLD MAN. No debt, son.

SAVAGE. And because one not-so-very-mad night I squirmed against his mother, to the ticking of the wedding present and the clatter of the drunkards in the sick-swamped street, so setting in motion the torture of paternity, **I owe no debt, me neither, do I?** (*Pause.*) Argue. Argue for your rights to me.

OLD MAN. No rights.

SAVAGE. No rights . . . (THE OLD MAN *turns to leave again.*) And what is intimacy anyway?

OLD MAN. Search me . . .

SAVAGE. I clung to her and it was two pebbles clashing. (THE OLD MAN *looks.*) When I was in her, hard against her womb, some razor slashed my head, some miniature blade designed to kill conception **you don't expect to find knives in there of all places.** Anyway, it failed, and he was born . . .

OLD MAN (*nodding after* THE BOY). Football today, is it? (*A hiatus of pity.*) Did I ever thank you for the books?

SAVAGE. Books?

OLD MAN. On Homeric Metre. By Dr Savage of the University. To My Father on that great big empty page.

SAVAGE. Christ knows why I –

OLD MAN. An Introduction to the Iliad. In Memory of My Mother.

SAVAGE. Barmy reflex of a clever son –

OLD MAN. No, I –

SAVAGE. **Don't lick feeling off that line of arid print.** (*Pause.*)

OLD MAN. Wha'? (*Pause.*)

SAVAGE. The binding was so poor the leaves fell out. As if they were ashamed to hang with such a dedication –

OLD MAN. Wha'?

SAVAGE. **The sentimental liar I have been.**

OLD MAN. Kind thought I thought . . .

SAVAGE. Kind thought? I hated you. Your mundane opinions. Your repetition of half-truths. Straddling my back. You burden. You dead weight. **He's gone so why don't you.** (THE OLD MAN *turns.*) No one is here for long. Who knows, some death might be already on me. Some growth in the dark, deep wet. Give us some time for my own needs.

[102]

Old bones. Old pelt. (THE OLD MAN *withdraws some yards behind* SAVAGE, *and sits.*) We can have knowledge, but not in passivity. Knowledge exists, but the path is strewn with obstacles. (THE OLD MAN *breaks the plate.*) These obstacles we ourselves erect. (*He takes a shard.*) The conspiracy of the ignorant against the visionary can be broken only by the ruthless intellect. (*He undoes his vest.*) Pity also is a regime. (*He attempts to cut his throat.*) And consideration a manacle.

OLD MAN. Trying . . .

SAVAGE. Manners –

OLD MAN. Trying . . .

SAVAGE. Loyalty –

OLD MAN. Trying, fuck it –

SAVAGE. Responsibility, **iron bands on the brain.** (HOGBIN *enters with a book.*)

HOGBIN. Helen was a whore in any case, it says – (*He sees* THE OLD MAN.) Oi.

SAVAGE. **Knowledge is beyond kindness you know** –

HOGBIN. **Oi!**

SAVAGE. Shut up . . . (THE OLD MAN *succeeds, gurgles.*)

HOGBIN. Hey! Fucking hey!

SAVAGE. I know. I know he is. (HOGBIN *stares at him.* THE OLD MAN *dies.* SAVAGE *suddenly seizes* HOGBIN, *in a horrified embrace.*) **Kiss me, then! My triumph! Kiss me, then!** . . . The death of my father necessitates the cancellation of our next tutorial.

It is in the ambiguities surrounding unforgivable behaviour – moral speculation at its least repentant – that tragedy claims its victims, for to some extent the audience for tragedy *are* victims – of their own curiosity. There is even, perhaps, a price to be paid for such witness, as for the inventor of it. When culture conspires against experience – in the best interests of harmony, perhaps – theatre's special facilities for imaginative discursiveness, its ability to dispense with the disciplines of reality, its self-sufficiency with invented languages, become vital resources for the protection of the private, the unregulated, the disassociated. In such a theatre, the potential for uncoupling the individual from a morally hygienic culture is obvious and threatening. Judgement is suspended, and *debate* – the end of so much dramatic enterprise – redundant. Tragedy's engagement with the forbidden denies the collective its rights over the material of drama; and its innate denial of the domination of deterministic, circumstantial factors in the life of an individual makes it anathema to the ideologists, leading, in Brecht's case, to the groundless accusation that as an art form tragedy belonged only to the dark age of Greek despotism, when in fact the Athenian audience was more practised in democracy than Brecht's own contemporaries. It is the horror of autonomy that bans contemporary tragedy – a horror of an art without claims to the truth, for truth in a humanist theatre is essentially verifiable, either by common experience (the idea of 'recognition' in drama) or by reference to researched material, the 'exposé' being the typical contemporary product of the humanist project. Truth in tragedy is not verifiable, and – in a theatre of moral speculation, banished to that area which the individual, in his solitude, affirms or denies purely by his relation to the actor – it is the performance which turns the audience from potential critics into collaborators and accomplices in an illicit act.

In a recent play – yet to be performed or, perhaps, given its great length, never to be performed – the central narrative is reduced further in scope than in any other play I have attempted, and the effects are designed to be achieved cumulatively by apparently unrelated digressions, rather than through the normal apparatus of story-telling. The play contains four speculations on the story of Abraham and Isaac, in which God, sheltering behind the identity of a vagrant called Benz, quotes the celebrated biblical lines in a number of different contexts. This is the second of the Abrahams. The old man, who is intent on committing a murder as an act of faith, addresses his son, who is apprehensive.

Abraham holding a knife. Isaac enters, stops.

ABRAHAM. I love you. And because I love you, I should not hurt you. It is, after all, a definition of love. (*Pause*). But not the only one. (*Pause*.)
ISAAC. Why is there a fire burning?
ABRAHAM. Another definition might be this. That love conceals nothing. That love is absolute in truthfulness.
ISAAC. And the knife, what's that for?
ABRAHAM. This truthfulness would include the fact of the wholly random nature of existence, which neither pities nor consoles. It is not love to conceal this. It is not love to plaster madness with the fiction of justice or rewards.
ISAAC. I can't stay long because my friend and I –
ABRAHAM. **A new love I have wrung from the very bottom of my life**.
(*Isaac stares*)
ISAAC. Are you going to the city for a . . . (*Pause*.) But never mind . . . (*Pause*.)

ABRAHAM. I felt, once I felt, oh, so shallowly, Isaac, that you would live, and marry, and inherit, and enjoy, and see, and own, and exercise good judgement – judgement partly learned from me – measure, criticise, and sometimes, complain. (*Pause.*) A fallacy permitted to all parents **But I honour you with deeper truths my son.** (*Pause.*) I tell you, rather, the savage and relentless nature of all life. (*Pause.*) What other parent would? What other parent cast aside the consoling lies of parenthood? **None I promise you.** Kiss me!

(*Isaac goes to him, and kisses him.*)

To share in this, to wade in this, absurdity, demeans the very soul.

ISAAC. I never heard you speak like this before and why the fire, it's hot today?

ABRAHAM. Always I smothered the evidence. In song-singing. In dance-dancing. In love-acting. And why? **That you likewise should be deceived?** No, this chain of deception must be snapped. And you – you are the link.

(*Pause. Benz enters, watches casually. Isaac perceives the drift and makes to escape, but Abraham has him by the waist.*)

This also is a love!

(*He floors Isaac and holds the knife prepared. Benz speaks.*)

BENZ. A ram is caught by its horns.

(*Pause.*)

ABRAHAM. What . . . ?

BENZ. Just there. Sacrifice the ram instead.

(*A terrible pause. Abraham releases his grip on Isaac, who rises to his feet.*)

ISAAC. Are you ill? Come to the house. You're ill.

(*Abraham sways, Isaac looks at Benz, and runs away. Pause.*)

ABRAHAM. Why?

BENZ. No reason.

ABRAHAM. Why?

BENZ. No reason at all.

ABRAHAM. **I have unpicked my brain for this!** (*He looks at Benz, painfully.*) How else could I assent?

BENZ. You cheated me.

ABRAHAM. Cheated . . . ?

BENZ. What sacrifice was it, when you convinced yourself that life was vile? It was a liberation you were threatening your loved boy with . . . (*Pause.*)

ABRAHAM. Forgive me, I do not understand what –

BENZ. Oh, they all say that!

(*Abraham stares at the ground.*)

You were to submit, in all clarity, in the fullness of understanding, to the wholly irrational act. You were to kill your son without the benefit of philosophy. You were to make no sense of the deed, but to endure the purest pain. For my sake.

ABRAHAM. Why . . .

(*Pause.*)

BENZ. No reason. No reason at all . . .

(*Pause. Suddenly Abraham launches himself at Benz and tries to strangle him. They stagger in an embrace. There is a cry off, from Isaac. He rushes in, seizes the knife, and plunges it into Benz, who falls. Abraham looks at the dead figure on the floor.*)

ABRAHAM. Oh, now things will be hard . . . Now we will have only ourselves to blame . . .

(*Isaac runs away, ignoring Abraham's call. He runs into a street in Rome.*)

There is, perhaps, nothing which might be characterized as sacrilegious in the liberal climate of contemporary Christianity, and the retelling of myth is a practice as old as art itself. What these imaginary histories are intended to create, however, is a climate of moral uncertainty. In the absence of any satirical structures (and it is worth noticing the continuing authority of satire in establishing moral norms in contemporary theatre) this permits an audience to shed its burden of carefully compiled certainties and expose itself to what is, in effect, the chaos of an experience in which security is absent. All the acquired habits of public performance militate in favour of unity of response and dispensed enlightenment. Far from being a place of moral adventure the theatre has become disciplined by its responsibilities – spurious responsibilities to the collective, to social progress, harmony and so on, which have effectively stifled its ambition and its potential for unpicking conventional wisdom. Theatre is appropriated by the forward march of common decency.

If tragedy is speculation on behaviour, a modern tragedy must entail a painful loneliness, for both the dramatist and the audience, since the old recourse to religion, or the social obligation to punish transgression, is the factor of unification that cannot be recalled – even by reference to the popular will. Only through the obligations of solidarity can the community play – a particular phenomenon of the last decade – make its hollow appeal to civic virtues. For the modern tragedy, division is not only the subject, but the *object* of the artistic enterprise. It is discord that must characterize a theatre in an age of populism, and the theatre company, dramatist and actors alike, must cease to revere themselves as articulators of social scandal, the *lacrimae rerum* of late democracy, or the paralysis of bourgeois life – the deadening inheritance of Chekhovian nostalgia –

and revere themselves as something else – for revere themselves they must, it is no longer an age for workshops and the journeymen who are appropriate to them. When the atmosphere is thick with sentimental homage to welfare and community, the theatre – ever the enemy of order – will speak in discordant tones, it will strike that bargain with impossibility that has characterized its best moments – flagrancy, outrage, permission, a privileged space for madness, and a filter against news.

I would like to conclude with a quotation from my latest play, *Ten Dilemmas in the Life of a God*, which takes as its theme what is perhaps the greatest transgression of all – impotence, in this case a sexual impotence jointly effected by a man and woman whose form of desire – much to the fury of family and village – precludes, abolishes, sexual union, and thereby prohibits the collective's prime function – reproduction of itself. The man, Draper, has been imprisoned for an apparently motiveless murder, but one which has served to keep him from the object of his appalling need. He comes home to the enthusiastic greeting of his sisters, and the suspicious regard of his lover, Paula. He reflects on the experience of gaol:

DRAPER. At one time I thought the whole world lied in unison to hurt me but all the gaoled think that we are so tender we are so bruised and gradually the louts received their letters me however never me never this was certainly a distinction this adamantine silence they pitied me and yet I was not diminished and wore this smile because I knew you loved me or not loved no the louts talked love no I lived in you with or without permission I inhabited your arteries and stalked your brain love no the very word a lout's word surely I thought I had abolished it but I lack consistency in all things but one and that's
(*He stops abruptly. Silence. The dog barks.*)
My (*Pause.*) **Don't let me out I said**
I was not sincere
Don't let me out
Not entirely sincere
Obviously I yearned the fields the meadows the trams etcetera obviously the faces of my sisters and the racing clouds yes those obviously but
Paula to resume with Paula
And they offered me a ticket to another place they do that they name five towns and I did hesitate I thought of their cathedrals yes cathedral towns they were some in the South some in the frontier district I might be sitting on the train now scouring the horizon for the spires to come into view but no I'm here as if I'm here notwithstanding and you know I love cathedrals

Back
Back
As if choices were
Back
A fiction of the inverately political
(*He gets up, goes to each of his sisters and kisses them on the head.*)
Forgive me
I could have been so much
Oh, what a life I might have
But I exist only to make love to this woman which (*Pause. A distant train climbs an incline.*) I never have yet and . . . (*Pause.*) May never . . .

Recognition as aesthetic paralysis
in theatre*

The artistic intention of humanist drama is the presentation of man
in the social context in which he moves and under the psychological
conditions which afflict him. It is a project of representation, a form
of mimesis which goes beyond typicality to particularity and whose
intentions, on the one hand, are socializing, civilizing or revolutionary
for the audience and, on the other, entail a discharge of conscience
for the dramatist.

The essential characteristic of such a form is the notion of truth,
a truth which can be validated only by an act of recognition.
Recognition is the governing principle of the dramatic form which
has dominated European theatre practice since the Enlightenment.
This moment of recognition is simultaneously the igniting spark of
the experience of the play and the certain extinction of imaginative
trespass. Thus the play exists within strict demarcations, and these
demarcations are set by the audience itself which is invited to seek
comparisons with the stage matter from its own experience, validating
it by its 'possibility' or 'probability', and thereby assisting at its own
intellectual and imaginative execution, perhaps a definition of 'entertainment' as a phenomenon. It is flattered with the false entitlement
to judge what it witnesses according to the degree of recognition
achieved by the writer and the actor. How successfully reality is
reproduced, how convincingly the actor imitates, how authentic are
the emotional states generated on the stage, are all self-maiming
critical categories the audience is encouraged to apply.

Each of these judgements, which places the audience in a critical
posture at the outset, is a wilful limitation of the experience of theatre
and a manifestation of fear of the irrational which inundates the
humanist mode; in invoking the concept of recognition humanist
theatre disguises its repressive instinct, disguising it as social responsibility, critical vitality, celebration or the carnivalesque. By making

* Given at the British Council Summer School, London, 7 August 1992.

the success or failure of a dramatic work dependent on the reproduction of experience from *outside* the walls of the theatre, subordinating it to the suffocating principle of *imitation*, humanist artistic theology severs man from his own malevolent nature, his promiscuity of thought.

Theatre might be viewed instead as a de-civilizing experience, a series of permissions to transgress, an act of indiscipline or a mutiny whose forms are inverted reflections of conventional morality or moral speculations given entitlement of expression by virtue of the physical and emotional barriers separating it from the world. A theatre is a privileged space, and a theatre without walls, either literally of the street or one rigidly determined by principles of recognition, is no longer privileged. The wall excludes the State, the police, the priest, but also the activist, the social worker and the revolutionary. A theatre without walls is a theatre that has forfeited its privacy, and privacy in an age of dissemination, access and populism, is authentic rebellion. If the theatre's walls once permitted the indulgence of bourgeois fantasy at the expense of knowledge, they now protect the freedom to imagine from the humanist regime of relevance and collective discipline. In asserting the right to privacy, the non-humanist theatre establishes its cardinal aesthetic – the autonomy of the work of art as staged *and* viewed, the discrepancies and disunities of the audience being as crucial to the experience as the absence of consistency on the stage.

Let me state here unequivocally that theatre is without use, is the abnegation of use–value, and defies annexation or appropriation, being neither a diversion from the tedium of common life nor a palliative for deformed social relations, and therefore it reconciles no one either to his neighbour or his fate. It is more likely to induce rage or melancholy, even a disposition to suicide, than it is to initiate reflective action or rational discrimination. Its nature is torrential, barbaric, non-evidential, its methods are those of plethora and excess, and by its very origin in simulation, theatre is an unlikely host for the ameliorative project of humanism and its hyperbole of truth.

To achieve the eruption of theatre from the repressive aesthetic of recognition requires, as I have indicated, a prima facie assertion of theatre as privileged space, adjacent to but not *of* the social world, but furthermore, the demolition of the portals of delight which are the infantile pleasures of recognition, and their replacement with the sombre doorway of *anxiety*.

Anxiety must be the condition of witnessing drama that takes moral *speculation*, and not social *imitation*, as its unfaltering objective. This tension is the effect of *failing to recognize* an action, a character or a type, an uneasy rocking of all popular cultural modes. In failing to recognize and, consequently, being unable to predict (predictability being a breach of the contract between audience and stage), elements of the unconscious are stimulated which are denied in humanist drama, elements of primitive and pre-social fear, choices of the instinctive and even self-destructive kind, the very sorts of behaviour which constitute the *unrealistic*.

In complete contradistinction to the humanist theatre therefore, the ordering of experience is posterior, and not anterior, to the event witnessed. This ordering of experience is made, it if is made at all, by the audience in its individual, atomized form, and not by the director or by the dramatist applying theories of production, laws of clarity or cramping objectification. The creation of 'sympathetic' characters becomes of less importance than the creation of dynamic ones, because to 'sympathize' is essentially to recognize, to pity, rather than to be implicated oneself. The dynamic character is one who commands attention, whose actions are mesmeric, impulsive and unlicensed, not insane but socially criminal, whose virtues are explorations, and not ratifications, of the normal.

The Unrecognizable Theatre is one of emotion, irrationality and beauty, not of order, discipline, or the collective will as shaped by the contemporary conscience. It licenses behind its walls and in its darkness the privacy of unsupervised emotion, and in the absence of harmony as a pervasive principle, a Utopian repression, it allows the possible to exist as a spectre, both horror and affirmation.

The theatre lies under a shroud

Conscience kills art as surely as pity kills love. This is the miserable condition of our greatest art, where critics, directors and dramatists conspire to instruct us in political responsibility. Brecht (mercifully without conscience) suffered a comprehensible lack of nerve when facing the impotence of drama at the spectacle of a triumphant fascism, and indulged the grossest simplification of complex psychologies for political ends. A less justified cowardice distinguishes the liberal humanists who manage our great theatres now, those honoured with the task of reproducing the national ideology. Any theatre offering further versions of *Arturo Ui* or *The Accidental Death of an Anarchist* perpetuates the old lie of identifying the enemy and leaving the innocent immune – political theatre at its basest. But the innocent do not exist and Brecht's weakest impulse only massages the idealist absurdity that the bad can be told by their uniforms (Police, Capitalists, Vegetable Market Crooks), leaving the audience to relax in the secure knowledge the indictment does not include them . . .

The Political Theatre remains what it always was – what it must be, since politics is the art of simplification – psychologically shallow and a trumpet call to actions no one will perform, a dutiful raising of conscience (if not consciousness) that elevates the dramatist to the preposterous position of The One Who Knows, for while there can be no Geniuses any more (egalitarianism could not tolerate it) and the Author is dead (he/she must be, in case he utters a forbidden thought in terms you cannot forget), the Great Researchers are always among us, telling us the truth on stage ('dramatizing') we are told we cannot discover elsewhere. Thus hierarchy persists, in spite of so much disavowal, because the theatre of Enlightenment requires its teachers, those who will promote the false ideal that the Theatre Changes the World. It never changed the world, of course, but at its best it complicated it, making action even less likely than before. This the Greeks knew long before Socrates, being practitioners of the thing Political Theatre runs headlong from, the thing that filled Brecht with righteous horror – tragedy.

Tragedy, unlike the Theatre of Conscience, requires no validation, nor can it be inspected for documentary faults, its truth or untruth. It asserts nothing in its own defence – not its therapeutic essences, its cathartic effects on social behaviour, nothing Aristotelian at all, and certainly it is anathema to the improvers of the social world, for even where it asserts collective values it can do so only with an ill-disguised bad faith – in a spirit of compromise, with an eye to the church or the State. Tragedy exists simply because the pain of others, and subsequently our own, is a necessity to witness – not to make sense of, not for a utility value, but as something for itself – which is not to say it is Art For Art's Sake, the forbidden, oh, so forbidden secret thing that dare not speak its name – it is Pain For Pain's Sake, and how we as a culture shrink from pain, how all political parties are cemented in the same pursuit and share as their highest slogan 'We Will Eradicate All Pain', how we obscure it, and make the fatuous giggle of comedy the deafening chorus of our age. We can unite on our dislike of pain. Tragedy, however, is the terror of mediocrity and progressive ideologies alike. It is about infringement, and about the Self. It dislocates the conscience, and damages goodwill. In mass society, it has to struggle to exist.

The masses cannot be served. Whilst it is the vanity of the entertainment industry to posture as the allies of the inarticulate, only individuals can be stimulated by a work of art, and only those individuals with *a desire for complication* (nauseous with collective truths and endless access to all things except the experience of tragedy) will find in it the ecstasy of moral uncertainty. The individual who aches to know suffering as an entrance to an unknown world will sit in the dark (crucially dark, to disengage from his neighbours) and watch theatre's unforgotten (though lying beneath a shroud of conscience) pact with illegitimacy. In contrast to the humanist play, or the socialist play, the Play of Conscience in its many forms, the tragedy demands you leave your morals at the door, for in this space (absolutely not the street, but privileged) the beauty of the actor is not blurred by urges to *educate, elucidate or edify* – the message is absent, the message is abolished by *obscurity* (in an age obsessed with 'accessibility' what greater crime could the artist and the actor commit?)

Oh Michael, Poor Michael,
Who thinks Art civilizes you . . .

In mass society, great art is never socially desired, for it declines
the offer of instant gratification, it defies the ordinance to entertain,
and repudiates the collective will. Modern tragedy, which I have
elsewhere described as Catastrophist, sins against the suffocating
burden of the Brechtian and Stanislavskian method, with their
narrowly conceived objectives and repressive pursuits of clarities. It
celebrates the complexity of motivation, it enhances contradiction
and extols *the beauty of language* against the naturalistic, populist and
mechanistic metres of the street. It proclaims the theatre as the
natural resort of poetry and therefore insists on a new acting. The
political dramatist is above all concerned with the narrow goal of
communication – the tragic dramatist with *complication*; the political
dramatist begins from the assumption that the audience shares
beliefs, the tragic dramatist from the desire to break the solidarity of
his audience into atoms.

The Theatre of Conscience paralysed the actor (he or she could
not be permitted to divert attention by his personality from the issue
under *debate*) and subsequently paralysed the audience, which became
under the Brecht/Stanislavsky/Royal Court schools seized by *critical
attitudes* – it found a way of witnessing theatre which endowed it with
false entitlements to *judge the material* (in the political play, the
argument must be presented) instead of experiencing the emotions.
It came to the theatre trained with critical impulses and anxious lest
the meaning could not be instantly induced – the enlightened
approving the approvable, fatigued by conventional truths, awash
with yet more pity for what it had already learned to pity, its
sympathies fixed in advance, wearily expectant (yet fearful for its
absence) of *yet another humanist platitude*. This was surely one of
theatre's poorest passages, when so much of its store of powers was
contemptuously consigned to *the aesthetic*, as if this category
were suspect, reactionary and decadent, when in reality it was the
journalistic impulse in threatre that had made it truly decadent.

Oh, Michael, Poor Michael,
Who thinks Art tells the truth . . .

The journalist had defeated the poet, but not for long, since the
instincts of theatre revolted against the endless *dramatizing of events*,

and in any case it could not compete with the swift technology of the entertainment industry. The great consensus of *anti-pain* dealt the Political Theatre so many blows, not least the blow of being itself *socially correct*, part and parcel of the great collective conscience (*Miss Saigon, Les Misérables*, impeccably conscience-stricken and humanist). The theatre, uneasy under the shroud, reaches for its banished powers – *pain, poetry, and the actor's voice* – and the audience, yet to be born, but stirring in its discontent, longs to locate there what it cannot find elsewhere, for theatre must be an experience distinct from other forms and not reproducible there. It must discover in chaos and in pain the substance of social disorder, for the irony of art was always this, that it lent power to the powerless by its embracing of the forbidden, not by its reiteration of collective norms. *Theatre for what, therefore? For nothing*, for no end, and for the silencing of all those dramatists who routinely declare, as if their art required justification, 'I wanted people to know . . . such and such . . .', 'I wanted people to understand each other better . . .', a modesty which hardly conceals the arrogance of the self-appointed enlightener. It is, like all great arts, for itself alone, and the tragedy is written because it cannot tolerate the strain of silence any more.

The state of loss as the end of a dramatic performance

The theatre of humanism, radical criticism and celebration seeks a single end, the reassurance of the audience, the satisfaction of the bargain struck at the box office between the purchasers of comfort and the suppliers of delight. The payment entails a dispensation from the actors to the audience in the form of *perceptions*. This is the gratification of expectations, the sordid currency of spiritual exchange, inevitably barren. I left with more than I brought in. My store was enhanced. I profited.

In the Theatre of Catastrophe the foyer has none of the hum which characterizes the stock exchange of entertainment. The end of the efforts of writer, director, actors, is a *state of loss*. Nothing is described here by the term *creative*, the discredited alibi of populist culture in search of a leisure which is ethically justified. The *State of Loss* describes a state of lost morality, an ethical vacuum, a denial, a rebuke to order, a melancholy and a pain. It is a revelation of the essential terror of the world, and an abyss. The ability of an audience to expose itself to these absences is possible only through the heroic efforts of the actor and the unflinching qualities of the text. Only by poetry can melancholy be made tolerable, and only the poetic actor can bear the audience through its pain. This pain is *necessity*. The Theatre of Catastrophe is not the comfort of a cruel world, but the cruelty of the world made manifest and found to be – *beautiful*.

Two Bradshaws*

Covington was strung in the quickness of her nerves, already dislocated at the opening. In her the revolt against Utopia was already running and discipline alone had maintained a ménage of political responsibility. Thus the fall of the theorists, like the fall of a forest, allowed a blaze of light into an overshadowed soul. In Kelly, duty and collaboration were beaten out of her, as the brain of a boxer is loosened by his bouts, first by horror, then by abuse.

Covington was wit by instinct, a thing hidden from a humourless husband, a private and treasured resource. Kelly invented wit from the spectacle of horror, a thing to shield her eyes. In these different actresses, the terror of Utopia was varyingly described, its eating of the instincts, its fastening on fear. For Bradshaw-the-man was the supreme intelligence of idealism, the compendium of arguments whose patient expositions are the silent score to every action of the play, the intolerable presence of the harmonious achieved by force and reason, abolition, exhortation and the ban. From this avalanche of theory Bradshaw-the-woman flees with an inspired shame – Covington taking her revenge with every sarcasm in a spirit of youth previously denied, Kelly less adolescent, the rupturing of a partnership wounding more and the shock to reason reverberating in a scarce-believing soul. Covington sang with a liberated temper, some beating of wings never unfolded. Kelly, unloaded, disassembling a life and a household, with all this onerous word implies. She had been a collaborator, so that her freedom was wrung only from strenuous will. Covington could only have been the victim of a genius's gaze, and consequently flourished on the roads as if vagrancy were natural to her. In both, the reassembling of the man was the pretext for his abolition, the breaking with a past whose lingering inspirations generated nothing in them but a ferocious pity smothered

* Julie Covington, The Joint Stock Company, 1983. Tricia Kelly, The Wrestling School, 1991. Bradshaw is the protagonist of *Victory*.

with contempt – an ecstasy of cruelty necessarily poured on the head of a lipless acolyte.

In both Kelly and Covington, a power of emotional truth alone could substitute for the text's refusal of staged 'developments', the method of exposition by motivation, sympathy or objective. Since the text forbade the familiar deceit of allowing the audience to feel 'they would do the same' under the circumstances, insisting instead on impossible circumstances and unpredictable events, Kelly and Covington plunged those reservoirs of feeling which the liberal/ Utopian theatre bans – as Bradshaw-the-man banned the incomprehensible from his Harmonia, making sex an anaesthetized androgyny which even Scrope finds inadequate to experience. In these inspiring performances, the will-to-life, which forever entails the undoing of conventional truth, was therefore primarily an internal excavation of illicit feeling which in its purity and cruelty possesses the beauty of all incompatible things; Utopia abhors the incompatible, which is the source of its inevitable staleness and savagery.

The idea of promiscuity in the Theatre of Catastrophe*

The Critical Theatre, which for the sake of argument I shall take to be that of Brecht, Shaw and the bulk of our contemporaries, is essentially a theatre of clear objectives. It is predicated on the idea of 'saying'. In the Critical Theatre the play 'says' something to the audience, and the elucidation of this 'saying' is the function of the production, the aim of the director and actors alike. The contemporary audience is now thoroughly versed in this method, and a party to it, by training and experience. So much so, in fact, that it brings with it the demand that the play should 'say' unambiguously – a demand which, if unsatisfied, leaves this audience with the nagging sense that the dramatist and the actors are guilty of an act of collective bad faith. Consequently, the Critical Theatre moves inexorably towards an art of anodyne humanism, in which the actors and the audience tacitly collaborate in an act of 'saying' and the theatre diminishes itself in pursuit of the limited objective of communicating an idea, albeit in the form of a narrative. Behind this lies the notion of the author as a 'good' man or woman, whose trade is principally the dispensing of wisdom and whose vocation is the creation of harmony.

In this collective deception, where the audience is traditionally ranked above the stage like benches of judges for receiving and validating the idea, and where clarity becomes a fetish, falsely democratic in its elimination of ambiguity, what the play 'says' becomes merely the pretext for debate – the play is a means, not an end. What occurs therefore, when the play says nothing? What chaos ensues when the text refuses to admit an objective and evades clarity? What nightmare awaits an audience when the time-honoured Brechtian/Stanislavskian contract is denied, the contract which has as its main clause the obligation to communicate the idea? This is breakdown, of course, in the essentially polite social relations of the contemporary theatre, leading to a suspicion that the dramatist has no

---

* Given as a paper at the University of Exeter, 10 May 1991.

[119]

morals and the actors are being misused. Under these circumstances, the theatre becomes not a locus for the restatement of collectively-approved positions – hostility to war, hatred of exploitation, the rights of women – not a place in other words, for the rehearsal of humanist platitudes – but a site, or a landscape, for a morally promiscuous journey in which – since there is no objective – the detours are likely to be as significant as the route itself. The single most important consequence of such a mutiny against governing principles is the overthrow of the audience.

The notion of the audience as an indivisible authority with rights of judgement over works of imagination is central to the Critical Theatre, but it is an authority only so long as the dramatist regards himself as tutor, enlightener, truth-teller. If he or she refuses to plead an argument, and offers instead the spectacle of a free imagination disciplined not by morality but by an aesthetic of language and vision the audience is obliged to approach the work with neither power nor contempt – it is not under these circumstances anything strictly 'truthful' that is on show, there is no criterion from politics or consensus against which it can be judged. The net effect of this is that the stage acquires an authority over the audience, and in symbolic space this would entail the audience sitting on an inferior plane to the actor, who is no longer the didactic agent of clarity but something dangerously unreliable, something altogether more hypnotic and unlicensed. This is a theatre which abolishes debate, in which the play is a substitute for debate, and without obligation to notions of entertainment or enlightenment, neither 'delightful' nor instructive, it resolves nothing – on the contrary, resolution is anathema: it is tragedy without catharsis, tragedy in which the audience is implicated in the acts of cruelty it witnesses, and from which there is no relief or refuge in the reiteration of the utilitarian concept of the public good. It is, consequently, a theatre of silence and contemplation.

Given that dissension in mass society is almost an obligation, a theatre of promiscuity requires no special justification – indeed to talk of art requiring justification at all is one of the melancholy consequences of humanist culture – but its particular interest lies in its refutation of the *solution* as a moral category, for just as the Critical Theatre *says* the *idea*, it implies necessarily the idea of the *solution*, which is, broadly speaking, the elimination of pain as the universal objective of human effort. The humanist theatre, along with its

Marxist and Christian allies, poses painlessness, the elimination of tensions, as ideals against which the drama is judged; conflict exists only to be resolved. Art does not simply exist – it is annexed as part of the armoury in the struggle for human perfection. The narrating of facts in the researched play, the description of conflict or poverty of communication in the domestic play, the retailing of injustices in the play of issues, comedies of misunderstandings, are all essentially demonstrations of the possibility of the Solution for which the audience hankers, and which it pathetically believes it can discover in the mind of the dramatist. It seems to me there is a profound sadness in the relationship between the Reconciler – the dramatist – and the Seekers after Harmony – the audience – in the humanist theatre, a Utopian pathos which affects both Chekhov's appalling gift for renunciation and Brecht's hammering insistence that we can discover the Truth if we look hard enough. Even an idea as seemingly innocuous as Harmony hides within it the shadow of the torture chamber.

If the Theatre of Catastrophe willingly divests the dramatist of his divine status as dispenser of truth or harmony, and the audience of its absurd status as monolithic critic, what is it that constitutes the substance of the transaction between them? What is the theatre that has no Saying? Its method can only be the erosion of narrative, because narrative is itself the first element in the construction of moral meaning. What occurs in the form of consecutive scenes, or in real time played on the stage, inevitably implies a moral perspective unless the seductive effect of the stage is subverted, as I attempted in *Victory* – a highly narrative play but one in which intense imaginative efforts are made – by me in the first instance – to prevent the audience wandering into a state of dreamy sympathy with a preordained morality, the sort of Christian–humanist ethic that says all victims are good. Susan Bradshaw is relentlessly bad, even if she is a victim of political pendulums.

In later works of Catastrophic Theatre, I have attempted to deny narrative its authority by resorting to digression – certainly in *The Bite of the Night*, where time itself is also dethroned from its eminence, and in my most recent play, *Rome*, where the existence of one narrative is continually displaced by the eruption of others which only tangentially relate to it in terms of theme. I might also mention in this regard *The Last Supper*, the first play of The Wrestling School, which parallels one familiar narrative with parables of a completely amoral, and possibly incomprehensible, nature – or indeed, *The Possibilities*, ten related plays, which are simply scenes, on the theme of making terrible but necessary mistakes, the very idea of the Necessary Mistake being wholly inappropriate to the Theatre of Saying or a Theatre of Solutions. Apart from this disruption of narrative discipline, a second means of dislocation – and dislocation is the function of art in a time of smothering consensus – is the employment of the Chorus, which stands outside, and interferes with, the working of the Realist narrative, often in a form which refuses the audience the opportunity to take its statements for granted – I am thinking here of the wholly unreliable chorus in *Golgo* – but which also permits the restoration of poetry to the stage, thereby insisting on the distinction between the stage and common life. If the humanist theatre is essentially unpoetic, because it can only assert the collective language, the Catastrophic Theatre insists on the distinction between stage and street, and on the peculiarities of the dramatist's voice; it will not renounce its licence to speculate both on how things are done, and also on how things are said.

The question so often raised about all forms of artistic practice – 'how does this help us?', the anxious cry of the alienated in mass society – is best countered by refuting its very formulation, which threatens to diminish art and to render it as utilitarian as any other kind of manufacture. The Catastrophic Theatre cannot satisfy this mechanistic demand because its ecstatic possibility lies in its denial of the possibility of Solution. As a form of theatre it is so overloaded, so apparently excessive in language, metaphor, event, diversity of form and image, so promiscuous in its speculation, it denies the very concept of the ordered life even as an ideal. It is a non-Utopian art which pits cruelty against pity and recognizes their coexistence in the guilty and the innocent alike. Who could take sides when the court of Charles II exposes the spectacle of Scrope, maimed, in a wedding cake? The merciless humour of Charles II draws the audience into a conspiracy of his wit rather than into indignation at the fate of a decent man. It is indeed difficult to state whether any character in a Catastrophic play commits a bad act, so complex is the state of emotion which surrounds it. I have often said that the audience for this kind of theatre needs to re-fashion itself, since what it brings from conventional theatre merely excludes it from the experience – there needs to be a surrender of the critical habit, the value-assessment of the Brechtian school, the posture of offence, and, instead, a wilful abnegation of loyalties. So much contemporary theatre consists of the statement of loyalties, to gender, to ideology, to concepts of the progressive, even to melancholy, whilst the Catastrophic Theatre replaces loyalty with an aesthetic of will to experience – it discovers light in the unlikeliest places and air where it seemed at first impossible to breathe. It is my contention that the twin disciplines of entertainment and enlightenment have relegated theatre to a position of philosophical impotence, and that its much-vaunted ability to 'respond' to issues, its journalistic flirtations with research, have merely rendered it down to a classifiable commodity, a suitable product for the morality of a national theatre. In a promiscuous theatre, nothing is given or predicated, neither rebellion nor abnegation, and its aims are not to console but to stimulate a restlessness which is not – as in the classic tragic formula – discharged, but carried away by the individuals of the audience whose contrasting reactions to what they have witnessed divides them against themselves. I repeat that no one is educated by a play of this sort – no information, useful or otherwise, is communicated, nor is communication the essence. The actor is elevated, through language and through the extent of the pain he embodies, to a dominant status, one which obviates pity or judgement. The effect of this is that debate – the stimulation of which is the purpose of the Critical play – is abolished, the grounds for it subsumed *in* the production, rather than the production providing dramatized material to stimulate argument. The promiscuity of the imagination in the Catastrophic play, its unapologetic intimacy with the forbidden – indeed, the rupturing of the forbidden as a category – evacuates the territory of values. The production must become, in essence, a poem, and, like a poem, not reducible to a series of statements in other forms. In these terms, the experience of pain, which is the most significant emotion, is not viewed as a subject for amelioration, or abolition, nor made material for a moral argument, a pretext for Utopian aspirations, but is affirmed in itself, and for itself. The liberating of pain from its social subjects, and from its so-called objective conditions, is possible only in a theatre which is essentially promiscuous in moral terms, and, far from becoming what is inevitably described as 'pessimistic', affirms the individual's right to chaos, extremity and self-description.

[123]

E

On the sickness of the audience*

I talked about the sickness of the audience
The democratic indignation!
The froth of injured innocence!
One even threatened suicide if theatre did not save
The world
As if the people could be wrong!
And this cascade of passionate rebukes
Such as
Only a bad workman blames his tools
But who said the audience were tools?
They witness
That is their privilege
No
It's obvious an audience can be sick
If democracies can be
Mobs often are
It's time perhaps for artists to get off their knees
Audiences learn bad habits
Viruses affect them in their nerves
And maim their sensibilities
Wherever crowds assemble infections spread
Especially from critics
Those coughing celebration who are perhaps already dead
No you shouldn't come too near to these
And theatre managers with or without beliefs
From the access-mad and the I-have-my-rights bacillus
A soul might take a chill
And obviously from dramatists an audience might get ill
I spare no one
Certainly the sickness does exist
The symptoms can be annotated
The myopia of thinking all things must be clear

* The Birmingham University Theatre Conference, 1991.

The tumescence caused by the appetite for enlightenment
The unhealthy craving for laughter
The morbid horror of taking offence
The apoplexy of having paid good money to see this
The feverish ache for moral platitudes
The incoherent belief in the weakness of man
The low temperature requiring massage of existing beliefs
The proneness to falling into states of pity for others
The greater proneness to pitying themselves
The seizure of the muscles at the sight of pain
It is a list
Certainly it is now proper to declare
The audience requires a change of air

Eleven building bricks

1

The actor is a liar who must be credited. That much is obvious. But his lies cannot be modest. Who requires a modest liar? We go to be properly deceived.

2

The actor is a liar on our behalf. In the lies of the stage we punish the liars of life.

3

The theatre makes us ashamed of our sensitivities. Their shallowness. Their narrowness. The theatre mocks the dominating passion of our lives – self-preservation. In life we say always 'Thus far and no further, my sanity demands it . . .' In the theatre we say 'Thus far and further still, my sanity demands it . . .'

4

How weak it is to hear an audience was 'moved'. And even weaker to hear how it was 'informed'. Better that the audience was enraged, not from the antics of offence, but from the exposure of its hidden crimes. These crimes – the worst crimes – are crimes against personal experience. Theatre indicts the unlived life.

5

It was fear of theatre that made them drag it back into the street. They saw the crowd would smother it, as it aches to smother all seducers.

6

The audience asks to escape. But escape to where? Over the wall is another wall. It is probably no use to know this. The theatre's knowledge is not of the useful kind, however.

7

The theatre teaches nothing. Sometimes however, there is a plethora of teachers. It is better then to go to a dreamer, and if she misleads you, so what? You are misled. What is love, but to be misled from oneself?

8

'I did not understand the play.' 'You were not invited to understand it. We did not understand it, either. We merely believed it. Do you want to diminish all life?'

9

It was beautiful, but not in any way I already understood the beautiful. This particular beauty came in the guise of the ugly.

10

Theatre draws apart. It draws the audience away from its beliefs. It draws the social from the individual. It draws the individual from himself. At the exit doors, the audience finds it hard to sew its life together again. Some of this audience secretly hopes it cannot be drawn together again . . .

11

'Who wrote the play?' 'What was he saying?' Why must you seek to know his saying? It is the shape of his effort that constitutes the art.

Stages in the education of an audience

The resistance of the audience to what it witnesses works in our favour given

    the numb state of society

    the circulation of conventional wisdom

    the dearth of serious criticism

The audience comes to the new reluctantly and at differing speeds

It is unconsoled by a theatre of tragedy but learns to forgo consolation given

    society's obsession with comfort

    the political obsession with the elimination of pain

    the popular pursuit of pleasure

It begins to demand further exposure to the formerly unpalatable and in so doing

Recognizes theatre as the *solitary* source for spiritual pain since the refusal of pain diminishes the soul and this is *recognized* . . .

The relations between an affronted audience and the actor

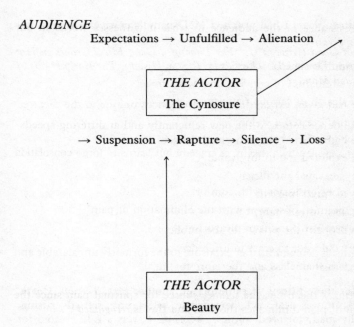

AUDIENCE

Expectations → Unfulfilled → Alienation

THE ACTOR
The Cynosure

→ Suspension → Rapture → Silence → Loss

THE ACTOR
Beauty

The anatomy of a sob*

For fifteen years I had watched McDiarmid's engagement with my texts.

That Good Between Us. The Love of a Good Man. Crimes in Hot Countries. Downchild. The Castle. Pity in History. The Early Hours of a Reviled Man.

He had given extraordinary performances unique in the theatre.

He had created a style.

He had married the body to the voice.

He explored the unforgivable.

He excavated the illegal.

He tortured himself.

He was unrepentant.

He brought the private to the public.

He would not tolerate indifference.

He was shameless and therefore mythical.

After these fifteen years he played another text, *Terrible Mouth*. In this, he was deaf, sick, voyeuristic, self-hating, self-advertising, sexually mad, tortured, pitiless, adoring. It was a role created for him, who loves the extremes. In this opera, he was required to sob. This sob he treated as part of the text and not a thing incidental to it. In it he saw not a momentary loss of articulation, but an opportunity. Always he seized the opportunity for other means of articulation – the seizure of an object, a garment, the annexation of things was part of his way as an actor. Here he found in the sob not a conclusion to an emotion, but the essence of it, and therefore

---

* *Terrible Mouth*, the opera by Nigel Osborne, libretto by Howard Barker, the Almeida Theatre, 1992.

brought to it that same excoriation and invention that attended on every line he spoke. He invested it with his physical resources as well as his mental agony so that his body struggled with the failure of words, as if words had been driven out of the cavities they inhabited – lungs, mouth, and arching throat – leaving gasping muscularity behind them, and into this vacuum flooded nothing but incomprehensible pain. The loss of language was like the loss of oxygen to a diver. Without speech his body writhed in dumb agony, desperate to articulate but betrayed by articulation, and in this silence he began to drown, for speech, as long as it existed, enabled him to thrash the waves of self-contempt and loneliness that plunged over him, but, speechless, he swiftly succumbed, a wreckage of jaw and tilted cave of mouth. He hung here as the unwillingly delivered sound of moral capitulation gathered from every extremity of his body, the sob which, overwhelming his reluctance, uttered itself into a silence of seized time. This sound was unearthly, recognizable only from the smothered pains of too-private life, or appalling memories of deaths and partings. It endured, and made one ashamed, as if one watched a secret horror through a pierced wall, which is also theatre and part of its power to discomfort us. Here was the hypnotic spectacle of another's pain, solitarily suffered yet giving strength, for what McDiarmid dared and triumphed in, we also might. There was a full ten seconds here, but such an anatomy of anguish one watched as if a cadaver were flayed before our eyes by skilfully-wielded knives, showing us what lay horrifically beneath surfaces, an écorché of despairing life. The sob was precisely a sob. In its sculpting, its unearthly musicality, it contained what we know from *within* a sob to be. It was experience exemplified, a testamental moment, gathering to itself the history of every individual witnessing it, and therefore the greatest accomplishment of the actor's craft.

The development of a theory of beauty for the stage

Supplied	Denied
Poetry and metaphor	Accessible meaning
Speculation on behaviour	Routine moral assertion
Psychological unreliability	Recognizable human types or political stereotypes with value
Complex syntax	Naturalism or Realism
Long speeches	Familiarity, broken exchanges
The eruption of alternative discourses *within* the speech	Narrative in the speeches
Moments	Objectives
The gaol	The room
The spoiled landscape	The garden
The cemetery	The market
Pain at the insubstantiality of values	Affirmation of values
Melancholy	Love fulfilled
Non-therapeutic	Functional rewards
Non-enlightened	Socially improving
Constant digression	Plot
Accumulation of feelings	Development of argument
Complication	Critique
Irresolution	Solution
Disintegration	Restoration of self
Impossibility	Recognition

Towards a theory of production

What is the theoretical basis of The Wrestling School? In its inception, its posture was oppositional, inevitably since it had chosen to dedicate itself to the work of an author repudiated by the national companies, but more than this, oppositional since what aspires to be new desires the annihilation of the old, and the old had anaesthetized theatre, making it a 'vehicle' for 'truth' when the School already doubted 'truth' and saw the play as a vehicle for nothing but itself.

Its starting principles related to the complexity of its chosen texts, the explosion of which dictated the manner of production and its values. These texts were texts of ideas perhaps, but, more crucially, texts of emotions. The emotional range of these demanded a special discipline in actors, since the Barker play never denies articulation, is not repressive, implicatory or suggestive but describes, expostulates, seduces, language is the means by which the characters repel the misery of existence, and in the beauty of their speech, through both poetry and abuse, will themselves new life. Speech therefore, the mastery of rhythm, the passionate plasticity of language, was its first requirement in the actor. These actors, in understanding rhythm, understood also meaning, for the rhythm released meaning. The actors were in this liberated from the dead routines of the domestic and the urban, reported speech, documentary speech. Their voices were restored to them and this alone electrified an audience for whom theatre's poetry had long been denied in the pursuit of a political aesthetic.

But speech had been exemplary before. What therefore did The Wrestling School bring to the speech that made it resonate beyond the actor's individual powers? The production of the play had to match the ambition of the text, which was not self-aware. Few texts possessed so little self-awareness, of purpose, function, intention or end. The Wrestling School text is for nothing but its own witnessing. It is too full for comprehension on any but the most emotional levels of perception. Only a pitch of emotional complexity could overwhelm the resistances of an audience educated in the disciplines of meaning and the habits of entertainment. The culture is not neutral, but flogs its publics into obeisance to governing modes, political, aesthetic systems of seeing, hearing, demanding. What therefore, could be the sufficient context for such plays as these, which denied at the outset the rights of the existing order? The reinstatement of beauty within a world of pain, the repudiation of austerity, the creation of visual metaphors whose melancholy lay essentially in a decay, and the aggregation of a musical score whose ambition gradually rose to equal the ambition of the text itself, give The Wrestling School a context of such sympathy that the violent, disordered, broken narratives of the production are unified, contradiction exemplified as grace, and the whole experience immunized against the cramping verdicts of a utilitarian critical ideology. Is this a fantastical theatre? Emphatically not. For fantasy aspires to the eradication of all pain, a drunkenness for the world-weary. The play of The Wrestling School requires nothing of the impossible, but insists on the far reach of the possible, its speculations far outstripping tolerance, its imagination too unstable for enlightenment. It proclaims the world unstable, but in the apertures of pain discovers beauty. The routine assurances of humanism are not to be discovered here ('Life's good for all that . . .') and death has powers banished from most arts. Yet it compels. The compulsion of this spectacle is its own morality.

Barely concealed irritation
– a critical encounter

Critic. Can we agree that the first duty of art is to communicate?

Dramatist. Not at all. Art has no duties, and therefore no order of duties.

Critic. Very well, but it must communicate, surely?

Dramatist. It does so, whether it aspires to or not. Any event communicates itself, even if it is senseless, the senselessness communicates itself. In the first instance, art exists.

Critic. Like a bus, a ship, an elephant exists?

Dramatist. No, because these are neither self-conscious nor contradictory. Works of art shimmer with self-consciousness, they are tentative, speculative, they create *anxiety* in the beholder. But they do not *will* communication, it is not a prima facie characteristic of their existence. That they do communicate something – almost certainly distortion – is an effect of their subjectivity encountering the subjectivity of the beholder. What strikes me as absurd, repressive and actually contemptuous is the idea of communication as *morality*.

Critic. So the audience is not to be catered for?

Dramatist. It is permitted to witness the work of art.

Critic. You make it sound like a privilege.

Dramatist. Exactly so.

Critic. And if it does not feel privileged?

Dramatist. It stays away.

Critic. It seems to me you do not value the audience greatly.

Dramatist. The audience are allies to works of art, but works of art do not exist for them, they are not the condition of the inception of works of art, which can and do exist without them. The absence of an audience from a theatre may condition a performance, but the experience exists, witnessed or not.

Critic. Perhaps you hold the audience in contempt?

Dramatist. On the contrary, it is you who implies contempt by assuming the audience requires the simplifications, recognitions and disciplines that constitute 'communication skills' in art forms. The infantile desire to 'communicate' conceals arrogance and patronage. I am thinking of imperatives to *clarify*, to *elucidate*, to *enlighten*, the prejudice that audiences are recruitable, molten masses in search of order and form which can be bestowed upon them by their intellectual masters. It is always the so-called Realists who are most anxious to package experience in this way, when we know that reality defies it. The primary and dominant relationship is between the dramatist and the world. The actor comes to the text that is the product of this collision, this misunderstanding (for all art is misunderstanding). The actor does not 'clarify' this, he presents it, in all its deformity, its lack of objectivity. He does so brilliantly, mesmerically, intuitively.

Critic. And he might perform in an empty room for all you care?

Dramatist. That is precisely the situation in which much brilliant work occurs. But the audience always exists for the work. It is actively in search of it. When it discovers it, it also discovers that certain rules of witnessing it are infringed. The audience is therefore under an onus to learn new ways of receiving it. It is not for the acting company to play new work by the old rules. This is a source of anxiety, obviously, and tension, even hostility. How else can the essentially problematic nature of the encounter be sustained? If it is easy it is meaningless, it is merely entertainment, massage, sleep-walking.

[136]

Critic. I find this idea of the theatre as a place of pain and frustration repugnant. I want to leave a theatre in a state of satisfaction, delighted and grateful.

Dramatist. What is being satisfied? For what are you grateful? I could propose a different set of criteria, such as ecstasy, wonder, the sort of confusion that accompanies the early stages of a love affair, sensations that are not inert as the ones you describe. In any case, how an audience leaves a theatre is its own affair and not a factor in the production process, which is concerned with creating autonomous works of art, not commoditizing imagination for a market.

Critic. When I go to a theatre I seek pleasure and edification. What's wrong with that?

Dramatist. You would not need to be a psychologist to know the source of pleasure might be the spectacle of pain. As for edification, the concept of 'learning' from the stage cannot any longer be seen as a simple process of didacticism. Artistic creation is so unstable that a theatre seems to me the last place you would go in order to 'learn' something. On the other hand, you might well discover something, but that discovery would be a private matter, the outcome of subjectivity stimulated by the incongruous or the contradictory. It would not necessarily be a moment shared with any other. I do not subscribe to the notion of collectivity in theatre audiences, it is another aspect of control, manipulation, even a manifestation of a corrosive 'goodwill'.

Critic. This all seems to me to boil down to an elaborate justification of obscurity. What is the use of something that cannot be understood?

Dramatist. What you characterize as obscure is anything that does not belong among the given, the visible, the tangible, the existent, the authentic, the apparently true, the recognizable and the familiar. A theatre that has no truck with the 'obscure' is like a game of cards – the dealing of known emblems and numbers, entertaining but enervating, predictable even in its unpredictability (the shuffle changes the order). Speculative art, which is ipso facto obscure, expresses not so much the *unknown*, as the *unannounced*. This is creative anxiety. As for its use, utility has nothing to do with art. Art is strictly useless, which is its rebellion.

[137]

Critic. Who would want to see work of this nature?

Dramatist. In the last analysis, it is not a want, but a need. The theatre must apply itself to a need, and leave wants to the entertainment industry. Work of the kind I am describing often leaves its audience speechless – there is a failure of speech to accommodate what has been seen, which is the confirmation of success in isolating itself from existing critical categories.

Critic. And this speechlessness, this impossibility of enjoyment, or accommodation, whom does it help?

Dramatist. Helping strangers is not the function of art. The theatre is not a clinic, nor is drama a therapy for social malformation. Are there not enough life-improvers but you want them to own the theatre? The audience that is drawn by this work comes precisely to escape the doctrinaire impulse you want to inflict upon it.

On plethora

The work of art is not digestible
but
overwhelms
systems of consumption
evaluation
use
repair

The ordering of experience
is
posterior
not
anterior
to
the event

Therefore the artistic experience
must be new
in form

In the era of
access
bowdlerization
democratic simplification
only
plethora
refutes accessibility

Plethora
is
the art of excess
made necessary by the
so discreet provision of subject matter
relevance
conscience
and
tastefulness

Excess is the enemy of taste
not tastelessness

In excess
theatre proclaims its divorce
from
the myth of ordered life

Too many narratives
too many digressions
too many themes
being the condition
of
willing surrender

The play of plethora
being a poem
cannot be reduced
not being
a communiqué
cannot
be
abbreviated
acknowledged
or
approved

It
is not a despatch from a battle
delivered by an actor on a horse
('the writer says to advance!')

But
a flood
breaching the dike
of
common experience
and
inundating
the ordered pasture
of
communicable material
(society)

III

A dialogue with David Ian Rabey

Rabey. Lvov's assertion in *The Last Supper*, 'Only catastrophe can keep us clean', echoes Bianca's line 'Catastrophe is also birth' in *Women Beware Women*, and Starhemberg's forcible tuition of Concilia in *The Europeans*. One definition of catastrophe is the experience of living beyond the point where death is preferable to continued existence, and I wonder how close this is to your own sense of catastrophe as potential explosion of spurious notions of life's worth or purpose, opening up tormenting roads to liberation. Your characters discover capacities to perform realignments in their selves through catastrophe which are incredible even to them, the phenomenon described by Helen in *The Bite of the Night* as the human ability to lose one's mind and yet find others, to lose one's sight yet see through other channels; and these characters are purposefully disturbing in begging the question as to how self-conscious or self-aware they are in their compulsions to excavate, explicate and perform their selves.

Barker. Catastrophe in my theatre is willed, as opposed to simply endured. Bradshaw's horror at her husband's quartering is only the beginning of a journey she undertakes. Her pain is a door to catastrophic experience, which she wills upon herself, almost as if she wished to expose herself to the whole range of possible disaster, and like a piece of wood or linen, to accept the warping which hostility inflicts on her. But the fullest manifestation of catastrophe occurs in the choice Savage makes in Act I Scene I of *The Bite of the Night*, the discarding of family, the passage of sacred barriers which inhibit knowledge. This is a rupture which is made in isolation from the external. His wife, on the other hand, seizes a catastrophic opportunity with the fall of Troy to deliberately lose herself. And others also interpret bad fortune as a concealed escape, for example, Bianca's reluctant acknowledgement of meanings attaching to her own ordeal, and a forced examination of her own sexual nature. And in *Brutopia* Cecilia exposes herself to the risks of insanity or violent death in her ruthless relationship with Henry VIII. What lies behind the idea of catastrophe is the sense of other varieties of the self repressed or obscured by politics, social convention, or simple fear. Bradshaw's journey is ostensibly one of piety – the collecting of her husband's parts – but it leads to acts of outrageous impiety. Savage commits impious acts as the condition of his tour. The will to be whole, and perhaps more than whole, is discovered in opposition to collective sentiment. Dramatically, the technique for summoning the will for this act of persistent rupture consists in constant self-description, the exhortation which found its first expression in a rudimentary form in Billy McPhee's last words in *That Good Between Us*.

Rabey. The most compulsive characters in your recent plays – *Women Beware Women*, *The Bite of the Night*, *The Europeans*, and *The Last Supper* – are self-appointed liberators who consciously inflict pain to stimulate. Is the willing of catastrophe on self and others the same as the impulse to tragedy?

Barker. The tragic resides in the refusal of the individual to leave the personality unexcavated, the eruption of will into areas of social piety. Savage's painful expression of secret thought, and the act contingent upon it, bring both him and Helen into the tragic arena. On the other hand conventional tragedy demands punishment for transgression – mental disorder or death. It is the revenge of the collective upon the savage ego. Savage is not punished, at least not by the collective, and Starhemberg defies the collective to the end, drawing Katrin with him. So these plays are not tragic but catastrophist. The tragic dénouement, the restoration of discipline over self by society or deity, seems to be in Shakespeare a neutered thing, a watery agency without vigour, unfelt and unbelieved. The punishment Savage receives is terrible loneliness, the effect of knowing too much. Starhemberg and Katrin discover new life through a love that can only be discovered in the extreme of resistance. As with Livia and Leantio, their claim on each other is conditional on rejection of reconciliation with the state. Lvov dies, but then he wishes to.

Rabey. A recurrent theme in your work is the body, its mutilation and forcible mutation by self and others; Helen wonders 'What joint or knuckle, what pared-down shredded section would be the point at which your love would say stop, *essential Helen*?' The drive to discover how much can be done to the human body before it ceases to be desirable, talismanic or powerful emerges as unsettlingly vital. The transgression of ostensible physical limitations and ideals breaks, by association, conventional socially restrictive notions of beauty, desirability, and endurance. For example, in *The Europeans* Starhemberg's ruthless adoration of Katrin leads him into rebellion against the aesthetic ideal of beauty which sends shockwaves into the State's ideal of order.

Barker. The body as conventional ground for controlled desire is one of the undeclared cornerstones of the State. It is inevitably associated with youth, especially with fertility, and effectively locates sexual charisma at the shallowest point. The freedom that some of my characters discover in locating sexual power in the frame of experience, e.g. pain, relates desire to the interior life rather than in the skin-deep fascination of the icon. Helen of Troy is described by Homer and all who follow him as youthful, beautiful, impossible-to-see-without-desire, etc., and Helen herself as reluctant, the victim of her appearance, and so on. But we know beauty has nothing to do with desire, and that a beautiful woman cannot launch a thousand ships, whereas we suspect a desirable woman might. This distinction is at the crux of *The Bite of the Night*. The state depends for its continuation on the cult of family and fertility, and fetishizes it by its collusions with the propagation of the beautiful, as thing to be possessed, as body owned and sold. I emphasized this in *Women Beware Women*, but also showed Sordido's ravishing of Bianca as the reverse of the coin. In *The Europeans* Katrin's atrocious condition is a spur to desire in Starhemberg, her eroticism lying precisely in her impossible-to-assimilate history. She has none of the functions of fertility, being unable to feed an infant. By loving Katrin Starhemberg publicly breaks the silent contract of socialized love.

But the body as locus of abuse and fetishization goes back earlier than these plays, certainly to *The Love of a Good Man*. The state has always played fictional games with the flesh of the dead. The Unknown Warrior is a response to the phenomenon of incomprehensible slaughter in the twentieth century, and designed to be an anonymous representation of sacrifice. In other words, the annexation of the innocent for the purposes of the State. I examined this proposition from a number of angles in the play. The symbolic and the actual coincide in the games played around the identity of a single corpse in the midst of monumental mourning. On the other hand, the State's ferocious dismembering of its enemies is of course the motor to *Victory*. The personal ache to recover the murdered, euphemistically called 'The fallen' in the Great Wars, but the 'criminal' after Great Revolutions, reaches its apotheosis in Bradshaw's theft of her husband's head from the sleeping monarch, who transports it about with him, a more powerful talisman than the works hatched inside it. This hypnosis induced by the presence of the body defies rationalism, as we can see in the supreme obscenity of Lenin's tomb. While you are a useful pretext for social policy your body is mummified. As soon as you are discredited, your remains are attacked. Stalin was turfed out of his mausoleum. His flesh had to be abused as well as his ideas. And this in the super-rational society.

Rabey. *Women Beware Women* and *The Europeans* depict speculative, disruptive actions which defy the sentimentalities of false democracies; these actions attack the ideal of 'kindness' by which populism discourages completeness of the self and the individual's will to know the true nature of his or her desires.

Barker. I have tried to open the idea of kindness to examination because it is so frequently employed as a ban on action, a means of stifling will and self-expression. There is a form of kindness which is nothing to do with 'kind' at all, but is a relentless charity which distorts the nature of the doer. Thus to be kind to one's relatives might be to stunt oneself, to be kind to the weak might stunt the ability of the weak to develop their own strategy and so on. Kindness becomes a form of oppression, enabling us to refuse courses of action on the grounds they might injure others. Against this regime of delicacy, Livia's ruthless setting of Sordido on Bianca in *Women Beware Women*, and Starhemberg's despatch of Concilia in *The Europeans*, are acts of calculated violence which are creative to both the perpetrator and the ostensible victim. I have tried in *Brutopia* to look for a creative form of kindness in the person of Cecilia. She looks for a truthful form of it, declaring she cannot find kindness in the company of the kind, knowing as she does her father's kindness to be the fake virtue of a Renaissance egotist. More was, in his political relations, a most unkind man, vituperative and merciless, whose Utopia is socialized oppression based on sexual abstinence.

Rabey. In *The Last Supper*, Lvov is an incarnate offence to populism in his completeness of self, when populism promises the provision of so-called 'essential' complementary elements and contexts which prove to be debilitating, intoxicating and addictive. I'm reminded of Nietzsche's identification of the herd instinct and its enshrined apotheosis in religion. You also seem fascinated by the promises and images of religious faith.

Barker. Lvov creates a religion out of denial, insisting always on returning responsibility to the individual seeker. He is never placatory and rarely congratulatory, making independence of self the first condition of freedom. He plays two versions of kindness against each other, knowing that only by repression are we able to perform acts of social kindness, whereas only by acts of self-affirmation do we achieve the other sorts of kindness, truth to character. The persistent acts of rupture he performs with public morality entail an isolation from alternative sources of power. It is paramount for Lvov that he will not play the messiah to those seeking simple moral consolations; the officer asks for a pacifist lecture and goes away empty-handed, as does the farmer, a sinner whose sin we never learn. At the end of the play, the returning officer, hardened and revolutionary, declares that those will be punished who did not make their messages clear – the first priority of power being the unambiguous repetition of moral postures.

I am less interested in writing exposures of religion than in describing the constant swing between submission and independence that religion generates. Sloman, after attacking Lvov for his refusal of democracy, cannot resist the man's sheer self-assertiveness, which he finds immaculate, and after a collective act of cannibalism it is he who asserts the unity of all who have participated. It is Sloman who is the potential high-priest of the cult. Thus his 'Hold Hands!' is both a cry of solidarity but also of mutual enslavement. The accommodation which the individual is prepared to make to sustain faith is inordinate, a kind of longing for servitude of mind, and this can be observed in the great rationalist religions also. When Gisela is brutally exposed to bad sex by Lvov, an attempt to break her loyalty, she manages to turn her very proper anger into a controlling pity for him, and it is a source of bitter frustration to him that he cannot break their will to servitude. But the best religious figures are those who are essentially corrupt, and know their corruption. As Stucley declares in *The Castle*, what help can the perfect be to the imperfect? Only the imperfect can help the imperfect.

Rabey. Whereas populism seeks to impose restrictive definitions of the self, the polar opposite force might be desire, which challenges even the *self-defined* limits of the self in a surge of derationalizing intuitive legitimacy, a liberation available to all yet defying generalization.

Barker. Passion destabilizes the character, and by extension, the social cohesiveness of the polity. It is literally incapacitating, which was why it has been regarded as an infliction or a sickness. But desire, reciprocated, directs energy and makes transformation both internal and external. Thus Ann and Skinner together can move mountains (*The Castle*) but Skinner alone becomes a monument to defiance, strenuously powered and a subject of desire in herself, who has no access to desire any more. The cult of Skinner and her wound, her terrible absence, lends her the prospect of real political power, but it is a sterile thing compared to her original state. On the other hand, there is something condemned about Ann's hunger for Krak, and his own dissolution in it. It is unequal and ill-fitting, and its cruelties are not creative in the way that say, Starhemberg's are in *The Europeans*. In all the relationships of desire in my work up until *The Bite of the Night* there is a stronger and a weaker element, whether it's Ann's weakness vis-a-vis Skinner or Leantio's vis-a-vis Livia. But between Helen and Savage there is a relentless and ferocious drive that finds a mutual inspiration, an inevitable passage of destruction.

Rabey. It strikes me that impulses to severance are crucial to your work – demanding the courage to act on one's love or hatred, or, most disturbingly, one's inextricably mingled love *and* hatred.

Barker. 'Impulses to severance' is a good phrase, raising once again the spectre of self-inflicted pain as a means to new knowledge, and yes, the hurt done to a loved one – and by extension, to oneself – is the supremely catastrophic example. This is difficult to articulate. It

[148]

is near to the subject that occupies much of my attention as a writer, the nature of the bad spirit, the meaning of wickedness. The rupturing of conventional pieties is a common theme in my work – Savage's murder of his father in *The Bite* (it is technically a suicide, but Savage demands it), Orphuls's killing of his mother in *The Europeans*, Cecilia's ecstasy in her father's death in *Brutopia*, all of them gateways to self-development but also appalling and traumatic. There is an earlier form of this in Bradshaw's conscious dehumanization of her son in *Victory*. What the characters do in rupturing these bonds is to create morality for themselves, as if from scratch. They insist on a carte blanche, however impossible. It is as if they were seeing their own lives as theatre, and demanding the right to invent themselves.

Rabey. The simultaneous co-existence of love and cruelty, or desire and pain, in your work is a more complex theme than can be encapsulated in the simplistic terms of deviancy, 'sadism' and 'masochism', in which social notions of deviance have their own effects of oppressive cultural (non-) legitimization. Lvov describes love as 'doing the undoable.' How might we distinguish love from desire?

Barker. To take the first part, you are correct to expose terms such as 'sadism' and 'masochism' as attempts to bolster a spurious normality in sexual relations. Not all acts of cruelty between lovers can be interpreted as sadism unless a real hatred of the other, as opposed to the profound resentment that lies at the root of desire, is the source of it. By resentment I intend this – the anger, and even shame, felt by the partner in the presence of the inextinguishable power of the other's sex – the spectacle of endless servitude (and ecstasy is a servitude) that sexual power (i.e. sexual difference) lays before us. This is a landscape of hunger which (like cunt in Krak's futile drawings) has neither edge nor width, and forever entails the abolition of dignity and even self-knowledge in the birth and rebirth of wanting. This resentment at servitude lies in the heart of wanting itself, and produces the ambiguous sense of despair and fascination which might lead to violence, a violence shared by both parties. Now, this is nothing at all to do with De Sade's monotonous savagery, where the orgasm is the single end of all imagination, and the attainment of orgasm an ever-diminishing prospect, available only by further refinements of cruelty. De Sade's violence is never mutual – it is not shared pain, but infliction.

The word love is not uncommon in my work, but I only edged towards a meaning for it in *The Europeans*, which is subtitled '*Struggles to love*'. And here it is in many ways not mediated through the body as desire is. What Starhemberg does for – and also against – Katrin is to insist on her right to self-description, resistant to the categories invented for her by the state and refusing the false reconciliations of History on the one hand, or parenthood on the other. His love for her is a love for her completion, her pursuit, which he perceives and perhaps judges more finely than she does herself. This certainly involves 'doing the undoable'.

Rabey. The Power of the Dog's subtitle, 'Moments in History and anti-History', seems your first step towards identifying a mythic power in individual pasts as opposed to national pasts. This power is increasingly identified with sexuality in your work, particularly in *Women Beware Women* and *The Breath of the Crowd*, which highlight exposure and realization of the unlived life, the uniqueness of each personal testimony and the sense of cumulative power involved in sexual encounters.

Barker. There is little or no aperture in *The Power of the Dog* for celebration or the catalogue of restorative things that are commonly associated with the humanist theatre. But what it does assert is the capacity of individuals for alternative experience and private history, which both dives under and is swamped by collective politics. In a world of Historical Method, blunderingly performed by Stalin with materialist rhetoric, an alternative fetishism is created by the dislocated, a viable private madness in collective madness. The image of Ilona, fashion model and atrocity-addict, is not easily prised open by psychological or political interpretation. She is a self-invention of the historical moment, absurd and yet powerfully evocative of wrong-rightness. In this, the play prefigures *The Possibilities*, which are all approaches to the idea of wrong-rightness. They are amoral plays, but powerful assertions of human imagination at the moment when reconciliation is a greater disaster than extinction itself. The willed creation of private history (Ilona's collection of photographs), its resistance to world-historical forces (an appalling category if there ever was one), and its insistence on private perception at all costs

[150]

(she will continue with her narcissism no matter what the objective conditions) come yet more defiantly in *The Europeans* where atrocity itself, as personified in Katrin, refuses to submit to absorption into historical material (the dead, the executed, the unknown warrior, the fallen, etc.) Katrin is the Screaming Exhibit, a phenomenon that rocks the Museum of Reconciliation. In all these plays, and, as you indicate, in *The Breath of the Crowd*, sexual history is made between characters with an authenticity that cannot distinguish their political actions. The dignity that is discovered in this struggle even lends a quality of beauty to the otherwise wholly disreputable. I'm thinking of Scadding in *Downchild*, for example.

Rabey. Your characters insist on absolute truthfulness, in self and others, in sexual relations, however harrowing the consequences. For example, Skinner in *The Castle* tells Ann to leave nothing out of her description of her relations with Krak, 'If I know all I can struggle with it, I can wrestle it to death . . .' Thus Skinner seeks relief from the self-torturing fascination of 'the imagined thing', which gnaws her to madness.

Barker. The demand for absolute truth in the sexual relationship is simultaneously the key to Skinner's evaluation to semi-divine status and a kind of emotional death. The truth is the devastation of hope. In a state of hopelessness she acquires the will to catastrophic experience, passing from passionate love-life to adamantine stoicism. As long as Ann remained untruthful, the possibility of reconciliation existed, though as a sort of half-life, the wanting in pursuit of the unwanting. But by submerging herself in scalding pain (the very last detail of infidelity), Skinner sheds a defunct self, a dead skin, and even seems to regard sexual madness as nearly comic, when Krak exposes his loss of self to her, his bewilderment in the state of passion.

Rabey. Don't Exaggerate, a direct address to the audience, seems a crucial development in locating obligation in the theatre audience on the specific occasion of performance. The prologues of *The Bite of the Night* and *The Last Supper* similarly emphasize the importance of what the witnesses choose to bring to, and give to, the theatrical experience.

Barker. The importance of *Don't Exaggerate* in my theory of theatre lay in its employment of contradiction and digression as means of returning the onus of moral decision to the audience. I now believe in the de-thronement of the audience, the abolition of its judgemental character, and the assertion of the stage over the auditorium. By this I mean the restitution of power to the actor, not as demonstrator of a given thesis, but as the figure who encourages the audience to abandon its moral and intellectual baggage and permit itself the greater freedom of an imaginative tour, essentially a destabilizing experience. The proposition of a moral posture, and its immediate demolition ('You exaggerate! You do exaggerate! You know you do'), has the effect of loosening ideology, implying the absence of objective truths, and forcing the audience to make its own decisions about the actions shown or described. What the audience is given, its reward for this dangerous exposure, is beauty (truth having been annexed by political or psychological theory). *The Last Supper* is beautiful in language and form (I am thinking particularly of the parable entitled 'The obscure origins of domesticity'), whilst being wholly un-ideological. The play is no longer a proposition about politics at all, though it is certainly about freedom. Rather it is a journey without maps and without clear instructions to the audience, which is sometimes pained by the absence of hidden orders ('Detest this character', 'See the manipulation here', etc.), especially when the character himself lacks stability (Ella in this play is both without words, then highly articulate, and Marya's contradictions are only superficially madness – they are in fact perfectly commensurate with frustrated dominance). In all my work after *Don't Exaggerate* the audience is unable to withdraw into the security of known moral postures. This alone serves to eliminate 'entertainment' from its experience, since entertainment is impossible without very firmly drawn demarcations.

Rabey. *Scenes from an Execution* dramatizes how 'artists have no power and great imagination. The state has no imagination and great power'. Do you think this relationship is essentially antagonistic, one describing the limitations of the other's reach and reference?

Barker. It seems to me impossible that the State and the artist should enjoy anything but a fleeting similarity of interest, usually in the aftermath of a revolution when the artist mistakenly believes his

[152]

imagination will be licensed as part of the cultural rebirth of a new order. The rapid restitution of economic and social priorities and the assertion of the collective, or its mediators, over the individual interpretation of society, make this inevitably short-lived. States are mechanisms of discipline, and perpetually involved in re-writing and re-ordering experience, annexing it and abolishing it in the interests of proclaimed moral certitudes. The artist, as long as he is in profound union with his imagination, inevitably finds himself opposing ideological imperatives and exposed to censorship. This censorship will always take the form of 'protection' of sensibilities (the weak, women, virtue, the family, our past, etc.) no matter what the ostensible pretensions of the regime – a left regime has to protect 'class' and 'reason' as well as all the rest, and is likely to be more restrictive than certain inert reactionary ones. Women have to be protected against abuse, and the family against its perpetual, but never total, dismemberment. The State is a mass of fictions held together by superior power. I believe this has been the case as long as the State has existed. The problem is to judge which fictions are necessary ones.

Rabey. How might the compulsion of audiences to witness transgression, as depicted in Jacobean drama, and your own, be distinguished from voyeurism? Can the stage release, as well as depict, the unlived life?

Barker. All descriptions and propositions of and about life in drama entail the possibility of imitation. But my plays do not operate as models of behaviour, recommendations or exhortations. They are not pathways out of collective life or manuals of mayhem. They do not attempt to demonstrate wrong life or detail paths to self-knowledge. Every play is provisional, just as every statement must be provisional. I have nothing to teach anyone. In any case, the pain and despair experienced by my characters hardly invite imitation, though conversely, there is no tragic dénouement which reinforces the existing moral consensus. Rather the plays remove, plank by plank, the floor of existing moral opinion in order to plead other, unarticulated causes. The audience (if there is such a thing, and since I do not seek a solidarity here, I ought to talk of individuals) feels itself bereft (and frequently exhilarated as a consequence) of its usual critical or empathetic equipment, and even insecure in its laughter, which is the last refuge of uncertainty. But this disarray is not sterile. Since there is a distinct absence of moral convention, the transgressor is not punished, the audience is obliged to arrive at its own judgement, not of situations it knows, but of ones it does not. What occurs in my plays is only partly life as it is known, after all. Mostly, it is unknown life. The audience is stirred at a subconscious level by the sheer volume of imagined life which the actors present. This is not voyeuristic, since it is not a fetishism around an observed action which leaves the witness transfixed but still hermetically sealed in his own moral posture. The possibility that is unlocked in the relations between characters drags the idea of hidden life into the forefront of consciousness. It is an acutely painful, and a half-reluctant, experience, to which individuals frequently return.

Rabey. When surrounded by normative systems of predictions, connecting with further normative systems of predictions, rather than with lived experience, one is in danger of being enmeshed in a climate of accrued debilitation – to quote *Don't Exaggerate*, 'the liars operate in the imagination, too'. But the subversive power of the imagination, and its address to an unwontedly full sense of human integrity, might reside in its unpredictability. In discovering integrity in action, the individual invents freedom for himself or herself in a non-ideological way, and becomes answerable to nothing and no one for validation. How close is this to the spirit of enquiry at work in *The Possibilities* and to your sense of theatrical surprise in general? Do the subversive powers of both comedy and tragedy lie in their demonstrations of essential incongruity? Is the vital essence of theatre a power of dislocation?

Barker. The hidden purpose of much modern drama has been the exposure of wrong life. The play states more or less overtly 'beware not to live like this', or in an age of ideology, 'you must put an end to this'. Both comedy and the sorts of tragedies we variously encounter conspire in this missionary intention. And it would be absurd to pretend audiences do not hunger for this instruction as vehemently as writers long to provide it. It is theatre's old obeisance to certain governing conventions. When the play fails to provide instruction in wrong life, unease is created and frequently, a piqued resistance. In *The Possibilities* I persistently refuse the answer an audience anticipates from the predicated situation. There is an element of frustration in it, but what prevents the witnesses of the plays from becoming vociferous in their unwilling subjection to the wholly unpredictable nature of the pieces is the peculiar, simultaneous ecstasy of recognizing the appalling strain of being human. They are not led or instructed by the story. The onus of dealing with the pain is theirs. There is no right course, or wrong action in *Kiss My Hands* or *The Philosophical Lieutenant*. Nor is there a generalized protest at the way we are, or our unkindness to each other. The audience suffers this, but the pain is somehow positive. It can only be that out of the deepest exploration of pain, unmediated by ideology or morality, a certain strength is lent by performance. The power of these pieces in production reveals the meaninglessness of the notion of 'pessimism' in art. It is not pessimism at all, it is the excoriation of experience.

Rabey. I know you resist sentimental or intoxicating celebratory invocations of 'community' such as some would identify as the characteristic cohesive effect of the theatrical experience – the descent (or imposition?) of communality which Hilton and others worship in mystical terms. Rather, you've emphasized the individual reflection of the single audience member, concentrating and witnessing in the darkened stalls. But what then is his relationship to his fellow spectators, and to what extent is this salient to the theatrical experience?

Barker. Yes, I am against the solidarity of the audience. It is easily manipulated and frequently, albeit unconsciously, authoritarian. The best moments in theatre for me are those in which solitary movements can be discerned, in which a sense of contest can be registered between the stage and the disjointed audience. These solitary contests are of course determined by the fact of the existence of others, they would be harder to achieve in isolation. The tension created by an assumed collectivity of response, which then disintegrates, leaving individuals exposed to the effects of actions on the stage, is to me a valid condition of experiencing art. The audience has to sense its moments of division as well as its moments of unity, which I would not deny, though I wouldn't locate this unity in the usual places, perhaps. The unity should surprise as much as the disunity. Often this sense of isolation is affirmed by the light of the foyer, where the normal buzz of the consensus is replaced by a

[155]

F

wariness to articulate what is still undigested. But I do not intend the individual to be without a guide. I come back to the actor, who by sheer bravery becomes the focus of hope and the source of security that cannot, in my work, be found in the usual forms of the message or the verisimilitude. In the actor's courage, the audience individual finds his own.

A conversation with Charles Lamb

Lamb. You're writing increasingly on theoretical matters about theatre in general and the social function of theatre. Have you felt it necessary to do this? Because it could be seen, perhaps, as a rather dangerous direction for a creative writer to take.

Barker. Anyone who has worked consistently at an art form for a number of years has a theory of creation and production. It is only a matter of articulating it that separates 'theoretical' artists from others. In my own case I undertook it as a work of self-defence. Unlike most ostensibly 'controversial' writers I had no critical support that was visible. Where it existed, chiefly among younger academics, and abroad, it couldn't express itself in the public domain. With the 'Fortynine asides' (p. 17) I recognized that the aphoristic was the most suitable for me, given the poetic nature of my writing style. But the theory changes, as the plays do in temperament and form. I have never thought it likely the style of my work could be dominated by a theoretical posture I had adopted, but rather the other way round. I am seeking to justify, in a post hoc way, what I arrived at imaginatively – that seems the only way an imaginative artist proceeds, blindly, wilfully, and chaotically, in the first instance, conceptually on reflection. But I was inevitably drawn towards questions of function and the social context of theatre. There was no theory of production which did not see theatre as essentially a critical medium. I was bound to collide with that.

Lamb. Two things occur to me: one is that there has been a tremendous dominance of theory in this country in post-war theatre, in theatre as studied in universities – I'm thinking particularly of Brechtian theory and the influence of Stanislavsky. This seems to centre on theatre being a form of communication which disseminates messages or truths to its audience. But the problem with your kind of theatre is that it doesn't do that. Derrida has said that the literary work should be 'insupportable', meaning not only that it should somehow challenge our tolerance but that it should resist analysis in terms of current theoretical positions – that it should not depend on or refer to theoretical 'positions' for validation, rather it should question theory. And in a sense it seems to me that what you're trying to do with your work involves a reversal of the normal assumptions; critics go to performances expecting to come away with something – theory, message or whatever; they do not expect to have their own assumptions challenged.

Barker. This challenge to existing critics and existing audiences is not a politics on my part, not a mischief, but springs – at the point of creation – from exhaustion with forms and assumptions, the obsession with clarity, for example, that I regarded rather early on as being a lethal ingredient in practice. After all, I never write from clarity, I have none, nor do I ever know the structure or narrative form, let alone the content, of any play I am writing. How could a theory of production that depended on 'clarity of meaning' and 'intention' have any relevance to me? Those who clamoured for meanings and messages were requiring the theatre to reiterate social propaganda within the framework of a governing social humanism, a compact of mutual celebration which had degenerated into massage. My first assumption became – a statement from bitter experience – that the audience and the stage are not united, rather that the theatre is a place of discomfort, and that its prevailing mood is one of anxiety. It occurred to me, almost as soon as I had emerged from an ostensible 'socialist' form of 'critical' writing (not that it had earned me any friends among 'socialist' 'critics') that – given the plethora of media information, social propaganda, collective affirmation, humanistic accord, that falls here like a drenching rain – theatre's only function now could be speculation, beyond the existing humanistic compact, in other words, for the theatre to become an illegal space. Instead of taking theatre into the street, as if it could speak automatically to all people, it should assert its privileged nature, its secret character, claiming privacy for the very reason that privacy in a populist culture is anathema and the subject of perpetual violation. In a sense, it should be hard to get at. Obviously this is the opposite pole from the national obsession with 'access'. But access is only control in another form.

Lamb. Brecht and Stanislavsky, and the notion of the play as having a 'ruling idea' seem very prevalent in the kind of director's theatre we have here. The theatre theory of the twentieth century pivots round the figure of the director – not the figure of the writer. And that shift is especially concerned with the exercising of a kind of control, the control of the performance.

Barker. That is true, but writers have conspired in this; since Brecht in particular, but it extends far back into the Enlightenment: also, they have conceived of themselves as civilizers. If you think your function is to civilize other human beings, you can't permit yourself the dangerous luxury of seeing the performance 'degenerating' into ambiguity, the actors playing contradiction, and so on. It is primarily a matter of disciplining the audience and the performers into a condition where they are able to 'receive' the dispensed wisdom of the text. In essence I believe the actor to be a symbol of mayhem, an unreliable reservoir of emotion, a licensed player of the illicit. Modern directorial practice has been to pin him to a rack of ideology – in the supreme interest of the collective, of course. He is diminished by this, and so is the theatre.

Lamb. I wanted to talk about the actor because the best response to your work has been largely from actors and I would have thought their response would come on a more immediate, experiential and instinctive level. Whereas the position at the moment is that your work is not acceptable to the major theatrical establishments, which are essentially directorial establishments.

Barker. Yes. I don't think it is possible to exaggerate the absolute seizure of the theatre environment at the moment. This seizure is the outcome of a peculiar collusion between liberal theatre directors and populist culture as a whole. The values of entertainment and the degeneracy of a critical theatre into a new sort of sentimentality have produced a theatre which is indistinguishable from other dramatic forms, but almost certainly inferior to them. It is my view that theatre has been good only when it disassociated itself from the governing ideology, that it made its business the experience of outlawed life – and I don't mean the fashion for criminality. The natural outlaws of society are artists, of course, and not criminals, who merely mirror the values of ruling systems. I'm referring to tragedy, which is trespass. Directorial theatre distrusts tragedy. It gets out of hand, is irrational. Most directors are uneasy with irrational qualities on stage, it gives them a sense of redundancy.

Lamb. Regarding the business of performance then, do you feel that there is a need for a new approach? One of the things that interested me in studying your work, considering it from the point of view of performance, was that it did seem to question the established functions of director and actor and the way in which these might approach the work of rehearsal and finally the performance itself. One of the things that struck me was the actors' insistence on the openness they found in your texts; so that when they went out to perform there was a sense that they did not know what was going to happen next. Now that sounds like nonsense because of course the text is there but perhaps they did not know what the motivations behind the words were going to be, what the implications would be, in which particular direction the ambiguities were going to tend or how another actor was going to play a line which they would then have to respond to. That openness interested me. One actress in particular, I seem to recall, did a lot of work on her part, examining all the different possibilities of the different situations but she would approach a performance with a sense that those possibilities were all still open.

Barker. This sense of fluidity – some actors might regard it as insecurity – reflects the manner of the production of the text itself, which, as I said before, was written in that state of chaos which I regard as normal with regard to my own work and life in general. Do we possess 'intentions' with regard to one another which are not in permanent overthrow? Do we not depend on a high degree of resourcefulness in our dealings with one another, seizing, abandoning projects, opportunistic at one moment, craven the next? The ambiguities that lie within speeches in my plays, the fact that characters proffer themselves, withdraw, exercise a desire, and even pretend to a desire in order to witness its effects, mean that both actions and speeches are ambiguous even to the character himself. An argument might be ridden like a horse by a character until a better presents itself – if only because argument in my work is frequently spurious, and only emotion is trusted, emotion conjures the argument out of need. Thus an actor will find it hard to lay down

[160]

a line on a character from any rational point of view, all he can approach at any given moment is the emotional demand generated by his character encountering another. This must change night by night, and no actor can ever play this work blindly, or soporifically, as they frequently do with texts which are cemented; it is also why members of the audience frequently return to watch again and again – partly to witness different aspects of the overwhelming density of it, but also to see performances in flux. This means the director's role is a different one. He cannot be the fountain of 'meaning', his autonomy is distinctly limited, and authority is widely distributed. His crucial function is to orchestrate. It is an aesthetic judgement that is called for here, a fineness of sensibility to the overall experience.

Lamb. One of the things that interested me in this connection is the business of bluff. It seems to me that quite a number of your characters in quite a number of plays are bluffers – they fake. And I feel that this is an important characteristic of a lot of performance. The ambiguity of a situation connects with this in the sense that you can have a character who plays a reaction which is – for want of a better word – 'genuine' or 'unpremeditated' – such as, for instance, pain – that can at a certain stage turn into performance when the character realizes the effect this is having on others and begins to exploit it. This is the kind of area where the actor actually has choices because at what point does the bluff begin and the spontaneity end? It struck me this was an opportunity for the actor to live the situation differently every time.

Barker. It is the reason why the work is violently unnaturalistic, for naturalism takes fixed character for granted. This acute self-awareness in characters is the absolute in tenderness, in thin skin. The word *bluff* implies a conscious manipulation, but this is not strictly true. The character is always governed by powerful desires, ones which are more or less permanently out of control, and therefore in crisis, he grasps, expediently, desperately, at whatever lies to hand, sometimes with yet further appalling consequences. Stucley, in *The Castle*, Charles in *Victory*, my Vanya in *Uncle Vanya*, nearly everyone in *Ego in Arcadia*, to an extent perform their own emotions and exploit the opportunities lent by their fascination. Stucley's long speech to his wife on his return is a tortuous series of attempts to

[161]

undermine her resistance to him, but they are not calculated so much as driven by need, a sort of brilliance born of panic. In this panic, a number of narratives are going on at the same time.

Lamb. Yes, that's a good example. You can actually have the opposite thing. Stucley performs his weakness – and he is performing, but he can also be seduced presumably by his own performance? And actually, although he sets out to control this whole thing from a strategic point of view, the performance can take him over and he can end up being taken back by it, becoming the victim of his own performance.

Barker. When the character expresses an intense emotion – released by the breakdown of stratagems or appeals – it flings open doors, opens vistas to new grounds of invention. The attack on the Bible and the Christian message by Stucley, for example, is primarily an expression of pain and loneliness, but hearing his own articulation of it provides him with a new resource. He attacks the Bible, he rejects it, then he retrieves it, annexes it, for his own purposes, by inventing the theology of Christ the Lover. The spontaneity of these emotional swoops forces him into new postures, so he does become both the victim of his emotions and also the shrewd exploiter of them. Characters therefore swing between control and loss of control. Naturalistic theatre is always bound by the possible, in effect, the already known. In Catastrophic Theatre, the impossible is drawn into proximity.

Lamb. Presumably this is where language is very important because the language carries the momentum of the drama and the characters, through using language, can be seduced by their own articulation. So there is a sense in which perhaps the words speak the character rather than vice versa. I think this is another area in which there is a problem with contemporary performance theory which teaches actions – the Brechtian idea of 'gestus' where one considers the action as a whole and the words are merely part of it. In considering the text, one looks at the line and decides what the action is, the motivation, and then speaks the words following up that particular action.

Barker. In such a theory, the words become of diminishing importance, they might even be incomprehensible, whereas I have argued that the power of language is crucial to the authority of theatre, but that it has to be continually reinvented: the dramatist must also be a poet, just as the actors must equip themselves to speak. The speech is specific to theatre, one of its highest principles and what most distinguishes it from film or television. In the speech the actor breaks the bonds of the real, disrupts the familiar, scattered syntax of naturalism, with its domestic associations, and draws the audience into a state of intoxication. It is the antithesis of critical realism, with its 'on the one hand . . . on the other' formulations, its commitment to objectification. And the speech does speak the character. Articulation in such torrents subverts reason, unbalances the complacent notion of stable character. In floods of temper or despair we say 'I did not know myself . . . '.

Lamb. Moving from the theory to the work that you are writing: it's changed very considerably over the course of your career – especially these last few years. But if I actually look right back through your drama, there do seem to be certain central issues and concerns which are remarkably consistent. In fact I was very surprised at the way certain situations which loom large in plays of the 1980s are there in embryo in plays of the early 1970s. How do you feel that the direction of your work has changed recently?

Barker. There are new themes, but also, as you suggest, themes which are entirely re-viewed. The idea of sacrifice for example, which could only be approached satirically in early plays, has taken on enormous significance in recent work. Smith is the first of these self-sacrificing figures, the first example of pure devotion that I have managed. Indeed, the whole of *Rome* is about the conflict between definitions of self and the abolition of selfhood. Then there are the servant figures who predominate in my more recent work, beginning with the servant in *Ten Dilemmas*, a man morally and intellectually superior to his master, but moved to terrible acts of service by pity, and the former tutor Dancer in my latest play *Hated Nightfall*, who converts a passion for revenge into a supreme self-immolation. Some of these investigations can be traced back to *The Possibilities*, particularly perhaps to the Groom in *Reasons for the Fall of Emperors*, whose infuriating self-abnegation is only slightly ridiculous.

Another theme which colours recent work, but which it now seems clear had earlier, cruder manifestations, is the idea of the insufficiency of the world, of the impossibility of discovering a place in it for those whose souls are, in a sense, too large for their environment, whose curiosity is too intense for the mundane necessities of social order but too desiring for solitude. This is very much the texture of *The Europeans* and of *Rome*, but you are right to say it appears embryonically in earlier plays, say, *The Castle*, where the emotional ambition of Skinner cannot discover an equivalent, or *Crimes in Hot Countries* where Erica is condemned to spiritual loneliness for daring to dream of her equal. This ill-fit with the world was solved in *The Europeans* only by a series of semi-barbaric acts of existential will, induced by Starhemberg, suffered by Katrin. The search for a reason not to commit suicide lies at the heart of my work, and what is distilled from that is a sense of melancholy. The most melancholic of my plays is perhaps *Golgo*, though *Ego in Arcadia* is profoundly melancholic. I don't mean depressing. Only a populist, entertainment-obsessed, comedy-obsessed culture confuses melancholy with depression.

Lamb. I remember you saying once that one of your major interests was character. You also said that you were interested in the point where the personal intersected with power and the political element, this latter coming to be seen especially in the shape of ideology. With this emphasis on the individual – and a lot of your characters are concerned to discover or follow their individuality – isn't this perhaps another kind of ideology? Where will becomes a thing solely in and for itself? I'm thinking in particular of the attitude expressed by, for instance, Stagg, the Home Secretary in *The Hang of the Gaol*, when he asserts the importance of 'clinging' – with all the negative connotations that word implies. Your political figures are often 'clingers' in the sense that they sacrifice everything to their will to power; and in this sense your political figures are, in their grotesqueness, perhaps your most conventionally 'realistic' characters. I suppose what I'm suggesting is that there is desire but when this desire meets with resistance it can be sustained by will and that at a certain point the initial desire evaporates and there remains only will.

Barker. The political figures might be divided into the active seekers for power, and those on whom power is pressed. If Stagg is the ultimate cynic of a discredited democratic system, with its honours and compromised loyalties, perhaps Skinner is at the opposite pole, one for whom political power is the ironic gift of resistance to authority. The former exists in absolute circularity. The latter is burdened with the moral dilemma of inventing a new system out of the ruins of the old, and the horror of it causes her to repudiate power itself. It is only when she perceives – in a spasm of pure feeling – her chance to indulge her appetite for revenge that she picks up the keys again. These are different varieties of will, one sterile, one passionate. You could include Toplis, Park, Lear, Livia, Ridler among the willed, driven figures who are both made and ultimately broken by their collision with power. There is nothing remotely ideological about these, if ideology means, as it must do, system, structure, law and inhibition. They are transgressive, morally innovative, insisting on a personal identity which the collective seeks to eliminate. This reaches an apotheosis in *Ten Dilemmas*, where impotence is reclaimed as a form of opposition, and punished. This is not a case of will outlasting desire – pure negativity. The self denies social manipulation, even if self is partially – and I would insist only partially – socially produced.

Lamb. This obviously links with another aspect of your thinking which is concerned with the feeling of being menaced by increasing social authoritarianism. I recall you once saying that desire would possibly be made illegal. How real would you say this danger is?

Barker. The political and social project of the twentieth century has been the elimination of pain, the elimination of conflict, the prolongation of life. The corollary of this is the promotion of happiness. Apart from regimentation, which has been tried, the best means to achieve these ends is to create a barrage of propaganda about harmony, and this requires definitions. Profound moments of desire are disruptive, because by nature they do not relate to given norms, they defy the definitions arrived at by opinion-makers, whether it be intellectuals or Welfare State managers, media bosses, or vocal minorities. The increasing level of social propaganda, disguising itself as news and information services, entertainment and the various sham manifestations of 'participation', eventually must locate its enemies, it cannot define harmony if its opposite isn't visible. We have experienced some of this in the identification and paranoia over 'abuses', which has clear undertones of the medieval, the witch-hunt. The resource one possesses to oppose legalized happiness is imagination, of course, but we observe that in the theatre – to take one example – it is distinctly subordinated to social realism, now an oppressive form, as I have said elsewhere.

Lamb. One of the things that strikes me is the quantity of common ground you share with the classical Greek tragedians where one finds the opposition of collectivity and individualism formalized in the division between tragic protagonists and the choruses: the former demonstrating hubris by overstepping the bounds, the latter tending to present conventional social wisdom. You have attempted to assert the value of tragedy in a culture which is resolutely bent on endorsing comedy as being both 'healthy' and moral. Though what comedy does more than anything else – as Bergson points out – is reinforce collective values and attitudes.

Barker. I identified some time ago the pernicious effect of the comedy industry on moral autonomy here – it is one of the oppressive social characteristics that appears like a plague in *The Last Supper*, and, as you know, I have regarded political and social satire as the essence of redundancy.

Lamb. Another aspect of this is that you seem to share the Greek suspicion of the idea of happiness. This mistrust is a constant theme in the classical tragedies – 'Call no one happy until he is dead'. I think most people today would find this obsessive or morbid. Perhaps the Greeks felt that there was something more valuable than happiness – beyond happiness, which they saw as illusory.

Barker. It is the social endorsement of happiness – its politicization – that renders it more oppressive as a principle of existence even than when it was first institutionalized by the utilitarians. It has become a 'right', along with numberless other 'rights' that a populist State vomits from its cornucopia. Because the Greeks understood the pleasures hidden in the spectacle of pain, as well as its place in life, its supreme irrationality, even its comedy, they did not resist it in the way we do, even though it horrified them. They saw the malice in things. We have never really come to terms with the Christian god, because he has repudiated malice, it is not part of his will, despite the terrible fate of Job. Inevitably, the liberal humanist State dare not contemplate it either, actions of ill-will can only be the product of social malformation, psychological disturbance, and so on. Malice was a characteristic of the Greek gods, so that ill-fortune was not greeted with the nauseating incomprehension that afflicts us, the rage at the 'unfairness of things'. Also, they knew as well as we do that the acquisition of an object, or a person, delivers rather little satisfaction. The heroic consists in reaching beyond gratification, in rendering gratification irrelevant. Thus the idea of being happy does not concern Draper in *Ten Dilemmas* – it is not part of his conscious-ness any more. That he is bound to a woman with whom he cannot experience conventional 'fulfilment' is a source of fascination, and fascination is the highest state a character can experience in my work – an abolition of ends, absolute desire.

Lamb. You have characters who transgress and who break conven-tions and taboos in ways such as we've been discussing but there are always consequences to these actions. One of these seems to be that the character comes to an increasing solitude; they are progressively isolated.

Barker. Not inevitably, though solitude is a state I cannot say I find appalling or contemptible. It would be a most unimaginative culture that could not see the virtues of solitude, or the reasons why one might opt to exclude oneself from society. Men and women have chosen it for centuries. It is true that the relentless pursuit of knowledge can lead to nothing else – it's the fate of Savage in *The Bite of the Night*, and of Park in *Rome* – Park is physically deprived of the means of communication anyway. It arrives to some as a consequence of their supreme powers of resistance – they become idols: who in *The Castle* can discover the means of communicating with Skinner, for example? And in *Victory* it is an irony that Bradshaw spends the remainder of her life with an enemy who has also lost the power of speech . . . though there is a physical intimacy there. This isolation is a testament to their heroic status. Some are able to suspend it – Galactia, in *Scenes from an Execution*, is prepared to submerge it in a dubious form of celebrity, Lear in *Seven Lears* is prepared to play chess with a cheat for his whole life in order to engage at some level with another human being, but it is primarily the erotic that provides the sole recourse . . . it is the erotic that enables Starhemberg and Katrin to overcome the blandishments of the liberal State in *The Europeans*, and the erotic subverts Ridler's missionary zeal in *A Hard Heart*. At a certain point, however, there is a transition, a triumph, where solitude is resolved into a moment of universality. I am thinking of the sacrifice that Dancer makes in *Hated Nightfall*, when he expresses desire in a form which precludes the erotic. He draws catastrophe upon himself, and upon the family he has been ordered to execute, as a gesture of spiritual independence: more than a gesture, it is a rebuke to a world in which both the reactionary *and* the revolutionary are decadent, intolerable.

Lamb. Is this what happens with Draper in *Ten Dilemmas*? Because he ends up in a position where he's more or less forcing the others to kill him but he himself pre-empts that by taking his own life. In that situation there were other choices available to him – he could have bluffed, or pleaded. So that would be an example of someone going beyond isolation into sacrifice . . . ?

Barker. *Ten Dilemmas* is a play about rebellion, in its most extreme form, ultimate rebellion. It is a rebellion against nature, against sex and against procreation. Death is inevitable, and the collective – in this case the family of Draper – are prepared to murder him in order to break the fascination that exists between the fecund woman (Becker) and the impotent man (Draper). Draper's self-sacrifice might be seen, therefore, as peculiarly 'responsible . . . ': Becker can do nothing but resort to another man, which she does in the last scene. But Draper's suicide is simultaneously the sacrifice required by the collective in full cry against a dissenter, and the act of a disdainful aristocrat who never for a moment doubts his power even if he suffers shattering despair. I cannot pretend to fully understand *Ten Dilemmas* yet . . . perhaps I never shall. In many ways *Hated Nightfall* is clearer to me . . . Dancer's lucidity, the defiance with which he sacrifices himself for a family who are not worthy of his sacrifice, is a perfect contradiction.

Lamb. We've talked about how you frequently present characters who assert their own individuality and are prepared to take this to excess, but you also show characters who do the opposite, who attempt to resign their individuality in servitude. Presumably you would not value this tactic of resignation of the will as highly as its assertion. Is it not as valid?

Barker. The idea of 'excessive' individuality is interesting. It suggests there is so much possible play in a personality that is submerged in the interests of order, discipline, political and social convenience, and if this is the case, then the theatre – as ever – poses the opposite, the unfettered, demonstrative ego. There are few victims in my plays – even the most resolutely punished of them all, Helen of Troy in *The Bite of the Night*, who is made the scapegoat for every failed system, turns her ordeal into a resource; her maimed body becomes an increasingly powerful talisman the less there is that remains of it. Armless and legless she remains an erotic fetish for succeeding generations. Katrin repudiates the idea of the 'victim' in *The Europeans* by thrusting her condition into the public gaze, an unrepentant hater. The victims of State power in *Victory*, Ball and Scrope, reverse roles: Ball becomes a silent, innocuous pet on a rope, while Scrope screams slogans at his tormentors. In a few cases, power becomes itself a tedium, and 'personality' a thing which, painstakingly made, loses its glitter. I am thinking of Toplis in *Crimes in Hot Countries*, Lear in *Seven Lears*, exhausted by enquiry, and the most potent example, Lvov in *The Last Supper*, a charisma at the end of its tether. Lvov has a household of 'servants', all of whom have renounced or try to renounce their egos in the interests of service to another. It is not until *Ten Dilemmas* that I dared to imagine the individual who yielded up his independence entirely to others, as opposed to the many characters who swing between submission and rebellion, as Lvov's disciples do. The servant in *Ten Dilemmas* is recognized by all around him as a man morally superior, intellectually superior, to those he has chosen to serve, who are themselves conventionally immoral. He does this from a profound sense of pity – not the lifeless pity we approve of socially, but a passionate love for two people engaged in a struggle *à outrance* with a mundane world.

Lamb. With your play *Uncle Vanya* it seems that you wanted to confront an aspect of English theatre which is reflected particularly in the popularity of Chekhov's plays. This is a kind of aestheticizing and celebration of hopelessness and apathy.

Barker. Works of art undergo changes of meanings from age to age, decade to decade. What I confronted in re-writing *Uncle Vanya* was the contemporary condition of the work. Chekhov may have thought his plays were comedies, but inevitably they have been annexed for other purposes, principally the endorsement of moral and sexual failure. The materialist argument that Chekhov was describing the decline of a particular class in the climate of gathering revolution may lend this moral weakness a certain documentary authority, but from the point of view of a living theatre, the effect has been to provide English audiences with an alibi for denying the speculative or the tragic. Chekhov, who seems to have hated the episode with the gun in *Uncle Vanya*, was so embarrassed by human action on the stage, as opposed to endless inaction, that he regarded this moment as melodramatic, shameful. I took this as my starting point for an unfolding series of incidents that obliged Vanya to reach for characteristics in himself that he could not normally expose, in other words, to lend him will. This castrated man is restored to his sexual powers and seduces Helena. Astrov, a fashionable ecologist, but still someone who cannot complete a desire, is murdered. The characters revolt against inertia.

Lamb. It's interesting that the shipwrecked Chekhov takes refuge in the room. In the sphere of theatre practice Chekhov is a very important figure – with regard to the development of Stanislavskian acting techniques. The 'system' could have been written to complement Chekhov's artistic vision – one of the striking characteristics of which is that there is no significant interaction. The plays dramatize the impossibility or worthlessness of this – as you say, it's a condition of negativity. So you have characters who are ceaselessly yearning towards each other but the play shows this to be hopeless and the only 'answer' is 'work'. The 'system' condones this vision by its emphasis on the primacy of the 'character', 'emotion' arising from the character's interior which serves to create an impression of the *role* as a precious but sealed balloon of subjectivity. Stanislavsky's 'system', like Chekhov, ignores the possibility of significant emotion being generated in and by the interaction of self with the other.

Barker. Yes, you have identified the crucial difference between my theatre and Chekhov's and between the Stanislavskian mode – with its domination of contemporary theatre practice – and what is required for my own practice. There is no carbonized stability of character in my theatre, no one is immune from the effects of others – on the contrary, the need to influence, subvert, annexe, seduce others is the very definition of existence. The consequence of this perpetual emotional imperialism or craving – it is a matter of judgement – is that action is the permanent state of affairs, that change is relentless, that the obligations of choice or denial cannot be evaded, and that selves are in constant play, every character has the potential for its own opposite. I have said often that the audience is – on an individual basis – given authority and autonomy by this sort of theatre, it is not trapped within the existent, not reminded, confirmed in its powerlessness. This dark, enclosed space, detached from the world, is a laboratory of human possibility. It has religious connotations, but whereas religion affirms disciplines, restrictions, theatre explodes them.

Lamb. A number of your plays – particularly recent ones – have contained clerics. And in *Rome* the central focus of the play is strongly ecclesiastical, involving not only individual characters but also the question of cultural identity as to exactly what 'Rome' is.

Barker. I think one has to examine the possibility that faith is one kind of freedom. We discussed the idea of servitude. What Smith performs in *Rome* is the absolute in priestly self-abnegation. She endures as literally as possible the ordeal of the man who has, stage by stage, become a god, just as God in this play manifests a terrible longing to be a man. Park, the immaculate Pope, is better at being God than God himself is, which is why he is condemned to suffer so inordinately. The reason Park has such authority is that he represents something superior to God – culture, 'Rome', the accretion of human artistic and social practice, which is in the end located in a fragment of a tea-cup. Smith's adoration of Park is inspired principally by his sexual pathos, but transferred to a set of values associated with 'Rome', few of which are ever identified: but that isn't important. What matters is her invention of an identity when social identity (the culture) is overwhelmed.

Lamb. The play is subtitled 'On being divine'. I'm interested in what your conception of the divine might be. Initially Benz is divine but clearly feels the need to engage with the human. He becomes engaged in a seductive deal with Beatrice which seems to propel him towards the human while she, on the contrary, overcomes what might be called her humanity – I'm thinking of her response to Benz's killing of their child. She says: 'There is the fact and the emotion. They come apart and in the gap's divinity.'

Barker. What is divine cannot be human, and what is human cannot be divine, therefore divinity is inhuman. We mean this even when we talk casually of 'divine beauty' meaning such exquisite beauty it is barely comprehensible, but there is a corollary to this, which is its moral detachment from human values. We know the Greek gods were without conscience, that the Old Testament God was jealous and vindictive, we even know that Jesus ran out of patience with the sick and tried to avoid them. We are frustrated by our own consciences and put limits to them all the time. This perpetual pull between the moment of authentic pity, which is rare, the trough of socialized pity, which is gesture, insincerity, public obeisance, and the violent repudiation of one's relations with others, which is a divine moment of moral autonomy, and of course, obscene if it were to become systematized, is the substance of the theology of *Rome*.

Afterword*

Do we have the theatre we want? Do we have the audience we want?

What is the meaning of 'we' in those two questions?

By what rights do 'we' 'want' anything? On whose terms? In whose interests?

The definitions inherent in these questions would be re-examined and reassessed constantly as part of the pulse of a vital culture. But it is hard to find any current debate of culture which carries through to ideas being tested in practical action, and even then the appeal and value of art – particularly drama, 'The Public Art' – tend to be defined and dominated by reference to an image of 'The Public', a monolithic restriction and distortion of possibilities, evoking characteristics such as habitual expectations and limited abilities in confronting depth, range, effect, change. Those who work in the theatre without conscious cynicism often feel constricted, compromised, even insulted, by having to diminish their engagement of efforts for this Procrustean spectre of 'The Public'. Some audiences and potential audiences do too, as theatre workers and audience members must have some human traits in common, surely?

Why? On whose terms? In whose interests?

Because drama is The Public Art it is usually implicitly interpreted as The Art of Solidarity. But – leapfrogging usual, implicit interpretations – what if a theatre located its aesthetic in addressing what lay beyond solidarity? Not everything that is 'public' can be identified as 'an act of solidarity' except by the most strenuous ideologue. 'What we have in common' is often invoked as our greatest sense of hope. The differences between us might be sources of hope, discovery and creativity also.

Theorists of drama, including Artaud and Brecht alike, make much of the submergence of the individual sensibility and ego into

* Originally published as the Introduction to the first edition of this book (John Calder, 1989).

[173]

a salutary corrective and/or relief provided by being united in a communal charge of feeling/thinking, the deliverance up of self to the reviving rush of instinctive entrancement or to the instruction of the greater yet humbler (because apparently anonymous) collective and its historical will. Such rhetoric of drama resembles that of sexual mystics who view the orgasm as a release from self rather than as a moment of profound self-consciousness. There is also a common implicit prescription of the sacrifice of the right to self-determination in the drama which 'takes you out of yourself' only to return you to the same essential shape, except more amused/enlivened/politically correct by virtue of this temporary release from the troubling complexity of individuality.

Howard Barker's drama centres on rupture, both external and internal, and the licensing of thought and feeling, instinctive expressions of human potential amidst its ubiquitous, often self-willed, restrictions. The writings collected in this volume are speculations towards a theatre in which audience members might be neither dismayed at, nor fearful of, the public expression or illumination of discrepancies between their reactions and those of their fellow audience members – and, indeed, discrepancies between their own reactions and their sense of what is commonly, socially right as a response, even perhaps what is right as their specific individual response. In this way, the theatre becomes a site of individual discovery, demonstrating the self's capacities for surprising moments of both intransigence and realignment. The unfamiliar permission of response, and the cowed, reflexively unified response it often provokes, is illustrated by this quotation from Barker's 1987 play *The Europeans*, where the Emperor addresses his courtiers:

> Sometimes you will want to laugh. And you will feel, no, I must not laugh. Sometimes you will suffer the embarrassment of one who feels exposed to an obnoxious privacy. You will feel, he should never have shown me that. And sometimes you will experience the terrible nausea that accompanies an idiocy performed by one for whom you felt respect. As if the world had lost its balance. I can only tell you, all these feelings I permit. So laugh when the urge seizes you, and then, be ashamed of the laugh. The Emperor only acts the insecurity of all order. Do you accept the truth of that?
> (*They shift uncomfortably.*)
> No one understands! Nihil comprehensa!

Indeed, audience individuals at a Barker play might find themselves capable of responses which are surprisingly shameless, as well as surprisingly shameful. Later in the same play, the Emperor proclaims the disturbing *aperçu* : 'No moment of unity is ever true!' (He is, of course, profoundly untrustworthy. So are all the voices surrounding him.) Alexander Leggatt identifies 'A fragmented world in which values are uncertain and the individual has to construct artificially a sense of his own identity – these are some of the basic conditions of Shakespearean tragedy'.[1] They are also basic conditions of Barker's catastrophism, which directly addresses the separateness of self in the breakdown of consensus. Barker has not characterized this separateness as necessarily to be feared, in defiance of populist sentiment of various hues and of attempts to ignore the breakdown of shared values and assumptions (as Jim Hiley has indicated, 'Liberal pundits don't like to be reminded of the collapse of the liberal consensus').[2]

Julian Hilton has implored of drama, 'If formal innovation is to succeed, it will have to break with the classical architecture of beginning, middle and end, as advocated by Aristotle, but also with the episodic theatre of the Brechtian kind. It must permit the possibility of moral and political meaning, but not depend on, or be circumscribed by, any single ideology'.[3] The rationalism – or more precisely pseudo-rationalism – so ingrained in twentieth-century British drama has impeded this innovation, remaining self-delightedly hypnotized by what Dragan Klaić has identified as 'the argumentative surface of rhetorics of conviction',[4] rather than being doubly disruptive of convention both in its address to unconscious and subconscious human drives and in its relationship between form and content (where form *becomes* content in experiential terms) – these are uncomfortable, because unfamiliar, directions for a drama striving beyond the dominant situation of the artist – self-consciously 'political' or not – and the audience seduced into pandering to expectations they have of each other, by way of the usual, implicit interpretations of The Public Art.

Barker's ambition to strive beyond past or present relationships between theatre and audience has led him to articulate and develop his own theories of how innovation might indeed occur, setting new terms for drama criticism and exposing the ludic regressions in the terms of the criticism currently written about him and others, with a view to advancing the argument; this collection aims to provide a concentrated focus and instrument of leverage to this effect.

In contrast to the confirmatory celebrations and deterministic didacticism which dominate and atrophy contemporary theatre,

Barker has rejected the reducible 'message' and, increasingly, the linear narrative, in favour of cumulative effects, variations on themes and contradictory experiences which rupture familiarities and conventional pieties to permit the release and range of the imagination. Incongruities, shifting identities, unpredictable events, with the disturbing power of a newly-forged myth, infused with the power of dream or nightmare – phenomena which are 'held together by connections which are emotionally powerful but logically inconsistent. Like life'[5] – or perhaps more like it than the omniscient air of pseudo-rationalist theatre, and with deeper and more persistent resonance. These are means by which form might, indeed, *become* content in experiential terms.

Barker's increasingly complex sense of character locates opposites which exist within each figure, so that there is no such thing as a stable character – any more than a stable audience, by implication; and Barker insists on exposing these contradictions, whatever confusion of conventional expectations (such as 'identifiable authorial viewpoint' or 'identifiable single message') results. His protagonists push their selves as far as they will go, no matter what the opposition or the awful discoveries entailed; his audiences are offered the chance to participate in and extend the discoveries depicted.

The subtitle to Barker's 1986 play *The Bite of the Night* – 'An education' – is a particularly felicitous choice, were one to interpret the process of education, not as systematic instruction or indoctrination, but rather as the challenge and development of intellectual, emotional and moral faculties: generating active thought in audience individuals rather than prescribing what they should think. This interpretative distinction between objectives is crucial in the evaluation of art and education alike. If only in this sole respect, one might make a connection between Barker's drama and Theatre-in-Education, another mode of drama intrinsically committed to the right of each audience member to work through and take away something different from the event, working through a method that is 'essentially heuristic', raising questions in the minds of its audience members that 'encourage them to reach for a change in their understanding', emphasizing 'redefinition rather than celebration'.[6] Elliot Eisner's distinction between educational objectives is salient here: 'instructional' objectives 'specify skills and information to be learnt'; 'expresive' objectives identify a situation in which audience members 'are to work, a task in which they are to engage: but it does not specify what they are to learn . . . An expressive objective provides [both actor and audience member with] an invitation to explore, defer or focus on, issues that are of peculiar interest or import . . . An expressive objective is evocative rather than prescriptive.'[7]

Numerous Barker characters lecture, expound and digress, challenging the audience to listen and follow. The protagonists of the monologues *Don't Exaggerate* and *Gary Upright* are the starkest illustrations of this, but it is also significant that Savage in *The Bite of the Night* is a professional lecturer whose activity has been legitimized personally and dramatically by his one remaining student Hogbin, one of Barker's equally numerous pupil or acolyte figures, who frequently voice probable audience unease or incomprehension at the teaching that is afforded.[8] For all the unequal power, both need and want the other as well as resisting them, testifying to Barker's recurrent interest in the dynamics of mutual challenge, and the paradoxical processes involved in forcing another into a position of autonomy, instilling a hunger which might oblige them to become their own invention: a theme analogous to Barker's own dramatic practice. Also, renegades like Gary Upright, Sordido in *Women Beware Women* and Starhemberg in *The Europeans* challenge by maintaining that others are imprisoned in mind-forged manacles to some extent of their own choice and making; and if attempting to engineer their self-release involves the renegades taking human icons like Bianca and Katrin to the edge of madness or destruction, then they appear prepared to do so, attacking individual happiness or gratification at its juncture with social equilibrium, indicating a painful, terrifying freedom which might lie beyond conciliation. These renegades take it upon themselves to involve others in agonizing confrontations with the bars of their figurative prisons; but it is the prisoner who has to choose to walk out through the ruptured door, and to embark upon their own programme of harrowing self-determination.

My suggestion of affinities between expressive educational objectives and Barker's theatre is not negated by his statement 'I have nothing to teach anyone'; in fact, he provides a startling correlation of patronizing, placatory attitudes in the assertion 'We are in fear of our own audience, as a poor teacher is afraid of the class' ('Honouring the audience') and refines the terms of the encounter: 'Rather the plays invoke moral crises which deprive the audience of its usual

[177]

judgemental opinion' ('Dialogue'). But beyond disruption, the plays also encourage the audience to reach for change, however difficult, in their understanding. This encouragement is generated by witnessing 'the doing of the undoable' – a challenge which occurs on two levels: firstly, on the level of witnessing Barker's dramatic characters undergo or submit to changes which defy our expectations or imaginings of what might be possible or conceivable for them to incorporate – and yet witnessing that incorporation occur, not only convincingly but compulsively; and secondly, on the level of witnessing Barker's actors undergo or submit to changes, in the course of representing these characters, which defy our expectations or imaginings of what might be possible for them or any actor to incorporate – and yet witnessing that incorporation occur, not only convincingly but compulsively. The sceptic might dismiss the occurrence of the first phenomenon as the barren fantasy of a romantic imagination, were the incontrovertible occurrence of the second not capable of achieving breakthrough, by which the occurrence of the first might be sensed as analogously, imaginatively possible. No wonder that some of Barker's most loyal and successful supporters and promoters have been actors; few dramatists issue such challenges, requiring such demonstrations of the paradoxical triumph of their craft, exploding and regenerating the configurations which, at any given moment, constitute 'human potential'.

The actor and director Ian McDiarmid, who has had a long and close association with Barker's work, asserts:

So many actors, by the time they are asked to play the great parts, are encased in such self-protecting armour that they are no longer equipped to play them. They lack the breath and the breadth. Instead of embracing the part, they find a way of keeping it at arm's length, of avoiding playing it. It is wrong for an actor to contain a part, he must open himself to all the facets the part contains. The central dynamic is to be found in the collision of the contradictions.

McDiarmid's comments on playing Shakespeare are also pertinent to playing Barker:

Naturalistic techniques are not appropriate . . . The plays aim for a distillation of life, not an imitation of it. Naturalism, or theatrical behaviourism, as it may more properly be labelled, is a formula, guaranteed to rob words of their value, to limit the actor's means of expression and deny those who people the plays their essential humanity and hence their universality. The act of acting is itself the articulation of an intellectual and emotional response. Therein lies its vitality.[9]

Rather than as a minister of solidarity, McDiarmid regards the actor as an 'archetypal outsider' who 'disrupts harmony and confuses morality'.[10]

Similarly, so many audiences, instead of embracing play or performance, find a way of keeping it at arm's length, of avoiding engaging with it; similarly, so many directors, and critics. Thus, actors, audiences, directors and critics collude in a self-compounding spiral whereby intellect and emotion are continually displaced by trivializing witticisms. Bernard Shaw's reflection on his days as a theatre critic remains enragingly pertinent: 'When my moral sense revolted, as it often did to the very core, it was invariably at the nauseous compliances of the theatre with conventional virtue'.[11] Thus is bred a theatre of insecurity, which lionizes conventional values for the attempted reassurance of those confined to perpetuating them, in an attitude of willed myopia.

On the other hand, the event of theatre might be the surprising confluence of various parties searching for knowledge, in their own ways, on their own terms, and finding themselves empowered to make new imaginative discoveries. Brian Bates:

> Personal knowledge leads to power. But it is not a power to dominate and control others, which stems from personal insecurities. Rather, it is the power to direct one's own destiny in the face of pressures to lead a life defined by the well-rutted channels. While the supposed aims of scientific psychology are to 'predict and control human behaviour', the way of the actor aims at self-understanding, which may render the person *less* predictable and controllable by outside forces . . . The way of the actor adds nothing to our lives. Rather it *takes away* ; blocks, restrictions, fears, boundaries and conventional views of the self and experience.[12]

However, it is worth adding that this demolition of the habitual adds, at least, new challenge; demands a reach of want to surge into the vacuums created by the demolished self-restrictions, and thus the process of self-redefinition begins, on the shoulders, as it were, of the drama witnessed.

Barker has emerged, unique in his generation and country, as an aesthetic–existentialist theorist who dares to match the disturbing power of Wilde, Nietzsche and Sartre, and dares to develop both classical and revolutionary ambitions into speculations towards new

[179]

theatres, new cultures. Beyond even this, his drama and poetry work in an arena, and towards an aim, of his own making and constant remaking: specifically, the soundings of profound personal difference by a central series of images or initiatives; and the very exploration of change, the dynamic which rips people out of their former selves, more alive but raw and bleeding, and impels them into a journey through uncharted territory where things and persons are constantly on the verge of turning into their supposed opposites: one's act of courage and faith might strike another as a bolt of the most profoundly painful evil. These collected philosophical epigrams and essays are pursuits of enquiry, challenging the theatre to anticipate its own identity, discover its creativity in new terms which might oppose their very existence to habitual associations, presented circumstances and the constraint of imagination by imposed status: arguments for an as yet non-existent theatre, which would thrive on arguments *in* the theatre as a manifestation of vitality, a mortar of change, beyond fear or shame. Rather than be stifled into mute or laughing inertia by deference to the myth of The Public, which has displaced courage from the centre of most theatres (On whose terms? In whose interests?), participants in the theatre which Barker envisions might separately express or discover disunity which, when publicly emblazoned, becomes beautiful and terrible, excessive and frustrating, wounding and splendid. Here, contrary visions of purity are necessarily and permanently at war with each other, as are different levels of self-knowledge and hope. Here, polarizations fracture, stability dissolves, and love and ruthlessness co-exist in the same person, in the same action. Authority and profanity split open against each other, exposing, in each, both fears and anticipations of possibilities of regeneration.

Notes

1 *English Drama: Shakespeare to the Restoration, 1590–1660* (Longman, 1988), 59.

2 *The Listener*, 15 September 1988, 42.

3 *Performance* (Macmillan, 1987), 152.

4 Conference on Terrorism and Politics in Modern Drama, 4–10 September 1988, IUC Dubrovnik.

5 Brian Bates, *The Way of the Actor* (Century, 1986), 136–7.

6 Charmian C. Savill, 'Theatre-in-Education in Wales', *Planet* 67 (Feb.–Mar. 1988), 49–54.

7 Quoted by Tony Jackson in *Learning Through Theatre*, ed. Tony Jackson (Manchester University Press, 1980), 77.

8 Other examples in Barker's canon are Downchild and Stoat in *Downchild*, Gaukroger and Pool in *Pity in History*, Toplis and Music in *Crimes in Hot Countries*, Sordido and both The Ward and Leantio in *Women Beware Women*, Lvov and the disciples in *The Last Supper*.

9 'Shylock' in *Players of Shakespeare 2*, ed. Russell Jackson and Robert Smallwood (Cambridge University Press, 1988), 47.

10 *Ibid*, 54.

11 *Three Plays for Puritans* (Penguin, 1946), 13–14.

12 *Op. cit.*, 9, 202.

Appendix: other works
by Howard Barker

Plays

Stripwell *and* Claw (1977)
Fair Slaughter (1978)
That Good Between Us *and* Credentials of a Sympathiser (1980)
The Love of a Good Man *and* All Bleeding (1981)
No End of Blame (1981)
The Hang of the Gaol (1982)
The Loud Boy's Life *and* Birth on a Hard Shoulder (1983)
Victory (1983)
Crimes in Hot Countries (1984)
The Power of the Dog (1985)
Scenes from an Execution *and* The Castle (1985)
A Passion in Six Days *and* Downchild (1985)
The Possibilities (1987)
The Bite of the Night (1988)
The Last Supper (1988)
Women Beware Women (1989)
The Europeans *and* Judith (1990)
Seven Lears *and* Golgo (1990)
Collected Plays, vol. 1 (1990)
Early Hours of a Reviled Man *and* A Hard Heart (1992)
Brutopia, Uncle Vanya, Ten Dilemmas in the Life of a God *and* Rome, *in* Collected Plays, vol. 2 (1993)
Ego in Arcadia
Hated Nightfall

Poetry

Don't Exaggerate (1985)
The Breath of the Crowd (1986)
Gary the Thief/Gary Upright (1987)
Lullabies for the Impatient (1988)

The Ascent of Monte Grappa (1991)
(all published by John Calder)

Opera

Terrible Mouth, music by Nigel Osborne (Universal Edition, 1992)